THiNK

WORKBOOK 5

C1

Herbert Puchta, Jeff Stranks & Peter Lewis-Jones

T0349715

CAMBRIDGE
UNIVERSITY PRESS

Acknowledgements

The authors and publishers acknowledge the following sources of copyright material and are grateful for the permissions granted. While every effort has been made, it has not always been possible to identify the sources of all the material used, or to trace all copyright holders. If any omissions are brought to our notice, we will be happy to include the appropriate acknowledgements on reprinting and in the next update to the digital edition, as applicable.

Guardian News and Media Limited for the text on p. 14 adapted from 'Experience: I found my identical twin on YouTube' by Anaïs Bordier, The Guardian, 10.07.2015. Copyright Guardian News & Media Ltd 2016;

Guardian News and Media Limited for the text on p. 40 adapted from 'Laughter therapy', The Observer, 06.07.2008. Copyright Guardian News & Media Ltd 2016;

Spin Solutions Ltd for the text on p. 45 adapted from 'Laughlab', http://laughlab.co.uk. Copyright © Spin Solution Ltd. Reproduced by permission;

Telegraph Group Media Limited for the text on p. 53 adapted from 'British skydiver makes first jump over Mount Everest' by Alastair Jamieson, The Telegraph, 08.10.2008. Copyright © Telegraph Group Media Limited 2008;

Guardian News and Media Limited for the text on p. 61 adapted from 'How many Twitter followers do you need to get a hotel discount?' by Trevor Baker, The Guardian, 02.10.2014. Copyright Guardian News & Media Ltd 2016;

Worldcrunch for the text on p. 76 adapted from 'Hyper-Polyglot, Greek Translator Speaks 32 Languages' by Christoph B. Schiltz, 18.09.2014. Reproduced by permission;

Peter Corning for the text on p. 86 adapted from 'What's Your Fairness Quotient?' by Peter Corning, https://www.psychologytoday.com/blog/the-fair-society/201108/what-s-your-fairness-quotient?collection=156411. Reproduced by kind permission of Peter Corning;

The Independent for the text on p. 94 adapted from 'Older children to start school later to find out if it suits their biological clocks' by Steve Connor, The Independent, 08.09.2015. Copyright © The Independent;

Juan Pablo Culasso for the text on p. 117 adapted from 'Welcome to the Atlantic Forest' by Juan Pablo Culasso. Reproduced by kind permission of Juan Pablo Culasso.

The publisher has used its best endeavours to ensure that the URLs for external websites referred to in this book are correct and active at the time of going to press. However, the publisher has no responsibility for the websites and can make no guarantee that a site will remain live or that the content is or will remain appropriate.

Corpus

Development of this publication has made use of the Cambridge English Corpus (CEC). The CEC is a computer database of contemporary spoken and written English, which currently stands at over one billion words. It includes British English, American English and other varieties of English. It also includes the Cambridge Learner Corpus, developed in collaboration with Cambridge English Language Assessment. Cambridge University Press has built up the CEC to provide evidence about language use that helps to produce better language teaching materials.

English Profile

This product is informed by the English Vocabulary Profile, built as part of English Profile, a collaborative programme designed to enhance the learning, teaching and assessment of English worldwide. Its main funding partners are Cambridge University Press and Cambridge English Language Assessment and its aim is to create a 'profile' for English linked to the Common European Framework of Reference for Languages (CEF). English Profile outcomes, such as the English Vocabulary Profile, will provide detailed information about the language that learners can be expected to demonstrate at each CEF level, offering a clear benchmark for learners' proficiency. For more information, please visit www.englishprofile.org

Cambridge Dictionaries

Cambridge dictionaries are the world's most widely used dictionaries for learners of English. The dictionaries are available in print and online at dictionary.cambridge.org. Copyright © Cambridge University Press, reproduced with permission.

The publishers are grateful to the following for permission to reproduce copyright photographs and material:

T = Top, B = Below, L = Left, R = Right, C = Centre

p. 6: ©william87/iStock/Getty Images Plus/Getty Images; p. 10: ©oksun70/iStock/Getty Images Plus/Getty Images; p. 14: ©Dustin Finkelstein/Getty Images for SXSW; p. 15: ©Alina Solovyova-Vincent/E+/Getty Images; p. 16 (L): ©Betsie Van der Meer/Stone/Getty Images; p. 16 (C): ©Patti McConville/Photographer's Choice/Getty Images; p. 16 (R): ©SVGiles/Moment/Getty Images; p. 17 (T): ©Uwe Krejci/DigitalVision/Getty Images; p. 17 (B): ©Daniela Duncan/Moment Open/Getty Images; p. 20: ©Tetra Images/Getty Images; p. 22 (TL): ©De Agostini Picture Library/Getty Images; p. 22 (BL): ©Kevork Djansezian/Getty Images; p. 22 (BR): ©Slaven Vlasic/Getty Images; p. 25: ©Brand New Images/Stone/Getty Images; p. 35 (T): ©N. Remond/Moment/Getty Images; p. 35 (C): ©Peter Dazeley/Photographer's Choice/Getty Images; p. 35 (B): ©1001slide/iStock/Getty Images Plus/Getty Images; p. 36: ©Iakov Filimonov/Shutterstock; p. 40: ©Pamela Moore/E+/Getty Images; p. 41: ©Vera Anderson/WireImage/Getty Images; p. 43 (L): ©John Rowley/Photodisc/Getty Images; p. 43 (R): ©Maica/E+/Getty Images; p. 46: ©Andy Stothert/Britain On View/Getty Images; p. 50 (L): ©flocu/iStock/Getty Images Plus/Getty Images; p. 50 (C):©Tom Szczerbowski/Getty Images; p. 50 (R): ©YOSHIKAZU TSUNO/AFP/Getty Images; p. 51: ©vuk8691/E+/Getty Images; p. 60 (TL): ©adventtr/E+/Getty Images; p. 60 (TR): ©scanrail/iStock/Getty Images Plus/Getty Images; p. 60 (BL): ©Cimmerian/E+/Getty Images; p. 60 (BR): ©scanrail/iStock/Getty Images Plus/Getty Images; p. 62: ©Jorge Guerrero/AFP/Getty Images; p. 67 (TR): ©Guenter Guni/iStock/Getty Images Plus/Getty Images; p. 67 (L): ©RyanJLane/E+/Getty Images; p. 67 (BR): ©Jason_V/E+/Getty Images; p. 68: ©Jay Paull/Getty Images; p. 71: ©GeorgiosArt/iStock/Getty Images Plus/Getty Images; p. 86: ©Kaan Ates/iStock/Getty Images Plus/Getty Images; p. 89 (T): ©Digital Vision/Photodisc/Getty Images; p. 89 (B): ©monkeybusinessimages/iStock/Getty Images Plus/Getty Images; p. 93: ©SilviaJansen/iStock/Getty Images Plus/Getty Images; p. 94: ©Yevhenii Khodchenkov/iStock/Getty Images Plus/Getty Images; p. 96: ©furtaev/iStock/Getty Images Plus/Getty Images; p. 98: ©Aaron McCoy/Hulton Archive/Getty Images; p. 99: ©Anthony Shaw/Hemera/Getty Images Plus/Getty Images; p. 104: ©hudiemm/E+/Getty Images; p. 107 (L): ©Andrew Findlay/age fotostock/Getty Images; p. 107 (R): ©Martin Wahlborg/iStock/Getty Images Plus/Getty Images; p. 108: ©Damian Turski/Lonely Planet Images/Getty Images; p. 112: ©LIBRARY OF CONGRESS/SCIENCE PHOTO LIBRARY; p. 113: ©WENN Ltd/Alamy Stock Photo; p. 114 (L): ©Yiming Chen/Moment/Getty Images; p. 114 (R): ©DC_Colombia/iStock/Getty Images Plus/Getty Images.

Cover photographs by: (TL): ©Stephen Moore/Digital Vision Vectors/Getty Images; (CR): © Tim Gainey/Alamy; (BL): ©Kimberley Coole/Lonely Planet Images/Getty Images.

The publishers are grateful to the following illustrators:

Bryan Beach (Advocate Art) 45; David Semple 6, 18, 32, 37, 70, 87, 106; Graham Kennedy 81; Julian Mosedale 4, 13, 24, 33, 54, 78; Tracey Knight (Lemonade) 72

The publishers are grateful to the following contributors:

Blooberry: text design and layouts; Hilary Fletcher: picture research; Leon Chambers: audio recordings; Karen Elliott: Pronunciation sections; Rebecca Raynes: Get it Right! exercises

CONTENTS

Welcome unit   4

UNIT 1 Brothers and Sisters	10
Grammar	10
Vocabulary	12
Reading	14
Writing	15
Listening	16
Exam practice: Advanced	17

UNIT 2 Sleep on It	18
Grammar	18
Vocabulary	20
Reading	22
Writing	23
Listening	24
Exam practice: Advanced	25
Consolidation 1 & 2	**26**

UNIT 3 Lucky Breaks	28
Grammar	28
Vocabulary	30
Reading	32
Writing	33
Listening	34
Exam practice: Advanced	35

UNIT 4 Laughter is the Best Medicine	36
Grammar	36
Vocabulary	38
Reading	40
Writing	41
Listening	42
Exam practice: Advanced	43
Consolidation 3 & 4	**44**

UNIT 5 Thrill Seekers	46
Grammar	46
Vocabulary	48
Reading	50
Writing	51
Listening	52
Exam practice: Advanced	53

UNIT 6 Followers	54
Grammar	54
Vocabulary	56
Reading	58
Writing	59
Listening	60
Exam practice: Advanced	61
Consolidation 5 & 6	**62**

UNIT 7 Beauty is in the Eye of the Beholder	64
Grammar	64
Vocabulary	66
Reading	68
Writing	69
Listening	70
Exam practice: Advanced	71

UNIT 8 It's all Greek to Me	72
Grammar	72
Vocabulary	74
Reading	76
Writing	77
Listening	78
Exam practice: Advanced	79
Consolidation 7 & 8	**80**

UNIT 9 Is it Fair?	82
Grammar	82
Vocabulary	84
Reading	86
Writing	87
Listening	88
Exam practice: Advanced	89

UNIT 10 You Live and Learn	90
Grammar	90
Vocabulary	92
Reading	94
Writing	95
Listening	96
Exam practice: Advanced	97
Consolidation 9 & 10	**98**

UNIT 11 21st Century Living	100
Grammar	100
Vocabulary	102
Reading	104
Writing	105
Listening	106
Exam practice: Advanced	107

UNIT 12 Unsung Heroes	108
Grammar	108
Vocabulary	110
Reading	112
Writing	113
Listening	114
Exam practice: Advanced	115
Consolidation 11 & 12	**116**

Pronunciation   page 118   **Grammar reference**   page 122   **Irregular verb list**   page 128

WELCOME

A LESSONS IN LIFE
Saying yes and adding conditions

1 Match the sentence halves.

1 I'll take you to the party as long ☐
2 We'll buy you a laptop provided ☐
3 I won't let you use my tablet unless ☐
4 Stop arguing about the TV. Otherwise ☐

a you agree to our rules about using it.
b I'll turn it off.
c as you give me a hand in the garden.
d you help me with my homework first.

2 Rewrite the sentences using the word in brackets.

1 If you don't promise to not tell anyone, I won't tell you my secret. (unless)

_____

2 You can borrow my phone but you mustn't phone Dave. (provided)

_____

3 If you promise to be back before midnight, you can go to the party. (long)

_____

4 If you don't turn the noise down, I'm going to call the police. (otherwise)

_____

get used to

1 Put the words in order to make sentences.

1 get / this / never / I'll / texting / used / on / phone / to

_____

2 new / few / took / used / to / school / me / months / to / It / get / a / my

_____

3 used / might / new / while / It / using / you / the / take / get / to / a / system / to

_____

4 Saturdays / got / early / on / finally / getting / used / up / to / I've

_____

2 🔊 02 Listen and write what the speaker says under the correct picture.

Love and relationships

1 Put the story in order.

☐ This time it was serious and they'd soon *fallen in love*.

☐ They *started a family* a few years later and that's when I entered the picture.

[1] My mum and dad went *on their first date* when they were just sixteen.

☐ They were married a year later.

☐ After a short time they *got engaged*.

☐ But my mum *wasn't really over* her first boyfriend so it didn't go very well.

☐ They started *going out* again six years later when they'd both finished university.

2 Match the definitions with phrases in italics in Exercise 1.

1 made a commitment to get married _____
2 a relationship _____
3 had their first child _____
4 for a night out together for the first time _____
5 was still quite fond of _____
6 developed really strong feelings for each other

_____

SUMMING UP

1 Put the dialogue in order.

	SHARON	I said I wanted to settle down one day and start a family.
	SHARON	Not really. She asked everyone.
	SHARON	Well money isn't everything. I could get used to having less money but I couldn't live without happiness.
1	SHARON	Miss Jones asked me today what I wanted to do with my life.
	SHARON	Well of course I do but only as long as it doesn't interfere with my family.
	TOM	That's a strange question for a teacher to ask.
	TOM	Well I hope you get what you want.
	TOM	So what did you tell her?
	TOM	But don't you want a career too?
	TOM	That's quite an old fashioned idea. Most people these days are more worried about making money.

B CHALLENGES

Verbs with -ing or infinitive

1 Complete the sentences with the verb given in the correct form.

1 meet
   a Tom's mad at me, I forgot _____ him at the station.
   b I'll never forget _____ my husband for the first time.

2 call
   a I tried _____ you but my phone was dead.
   b Have you tried _____ her home number? She often doesn't answer her mobile.

3 say
   a I really regret _____ those things. It was really mean.
   b We regret _____ that we cannot accept your entry for the competition because the deadline was yesterday.

4 take
   a Please remember _____ back the library books. They're due back today.
   b I don't remember _____ that photo but I do remember that day.

5 chat
   a Miss Green told me to stop _____ five times today.
   b I met Colin on my way home and we stopped _____ for an hour.

2 Complete the sentences with your own ideas.

1 I really regret _____ . I feel terrible about it.

2 Today I really mustn't forget

   _____ .

3 I must stop _____ . It's such a bad habit.

4 I don't remember _____ when I was younger.

5 If you're finding it difficult to get to sleep, try _____ .

Issuing and accepting a challenge

1 Complete the words then match the sentences. There are two extra replies.

1 I b ____ you can't eat all that pizza. ☐
2 I c ____ l ____ n ____ you to a race to the bus stop. ☐
3 Do you r ____ c ____ you could last a day without using your phone? ☐
4 I ____ e ____ I can finish before you. ☐

a You're probably right but I don't really care. I'm in no hurry.
b Ok, you're on. Last there pays for the ticket.
c That's too easy. I'm really good at swimming.
d Of course I could, but why would I want to?
e I bet I can. I'm starving.
f You'll never manage to last a whole day.

2 Complete the dialogues with your own ideas.

1 A Do you reckon you could

      _____ ?

   B That's too easy. I've got a really good memory.

2 A I challenge you to

      _____ .

   B Not now. I'm much too tired.

3 A I bet I can

      _____ .

   B No way. You'll never manage to do it.

4 A I bet you can't

      _____ .

   B You're right. Tell me.

Our greatest challenge

1 Complete the sentences with the words in the list.

apprehensive | feeling | believe | worried | positive | unsure

☹

1 I'm really _____ about my date with Dawn.

2 I'm a bit _____ about whether I should play in the football match after school.

3 I'm feeling quite _____ about the exam tomorrow.

☺

4 I feel quite _____ about my life.

5 I've got a really good _____ about the next few years.

6 I _____ things will work out for the best.

2 Add a reason to each of the sentences in Exercise 1.

1 *I haven't got anything to wear.*

2 _____

3 _____

4 _____

5 _____

6 _____

Phrases for talking about the future

1 Complete the sentences with the words in the list.

on the point of | about to | certain | off to | likely to

1 They are _____ the moon.

2 He is _____ lose his temper.

3 She's _____ reaching the top.

CITY 1   UTD 0

4 We are _____ lose this match I think.

5 They are _____ to miss the bus.

SUMMING UP

1 🔊03 Complete the dialogue with the words in the list. There are four extra words. Then listen and check.

apprehensive | certain | to do | about
to feel | bet | doing | right | challenge
positive | feeling | off

LUCY I [1]_____ you to come with me on the new ride.

ERIC What! You know how [2]_____ those things make me.

LUCY Come on. You've been on one before.

ERIC I know and I remember [3]_____ terrified the whole time.

LUCY Well I'll be with you this time. I [4]_____ I can help you forget your fear.

ERIC You're probably [5]_____ but maybe later.

LUCY We haven't got any time. The ride's [6]_____ to close.

ERIC We'll just have to come back another day then.

LUCY You'll regret not [7]_____ it if we leave now.

ERIC Maybe I will but I'm [8]_____ to get an ice-cream before the café closes. I'd regret that even more.

C EMPATHISING

Cheering someone up and sympathising about past situations

1 Complete the 'sympathising' expressions.

1 Don't let _____ .   5 How _____ .
2 What a _____ .   6 Hang _____ .
3 Poor _____ ,   7 Oh _____ .
4 Cheer _____ .   8 Look on _____ .

2 Complete the mini-dialogues with your own ideas.

1 A _____
   B Oh dear. I hope he'll buy you another one.

2 A _____
   B What a shame. And you worked so hard for it.

3 A _____
   B How terrible. I know how much you were looking forward to it.

4 A _____
   B Hang in there. I'm sure he'll get better soon.

5 A _____
   B Don't let it get you down. There are hundreds of other things you can do.

6 A _____
   B Look on the bright side. At least you saved yourself a few hundred pounds!

Life's ups and downs

1 Complete the sentences with the phrases in the list.

let her down | my way | getting in the way of
didn't live up to my expectations
tried my hardest | blame

1 That film was terrible. It certainly
   _____ .

2 I _____ to
   apologise but she just wouldn't listen to me.

3 There's nobody to _____
   _____ but yourself.

4 I can't believe you forgot. She was really looking forward to your visit. You really
   _____ .

5 Nothing's going _____
   _____ today. I should have stayed in bed.

6 These emails are really _____
   _____ my work.

2 Complete the mini-dialogues with the sentences in Exercise 1.

DIALOGUE 1
DAN   What's up with you? You've burnt your toast and spilled your coffee!
WENDY   ☐

DIALOGUE 2
PETE   Mum, I haven't done my homework. The teacher's going to kill me.
MUM   ☐

DIALOGUE 3
CLAUDIA Well, that was a massive disappointment!
TIM   Really? I thought it was good.
CLAUDIA ☐

DIALOGUE 4
LUCY   Hi, Mum. I'm home.
MUM   But you were supposed to go to your grandmother's.
LUCY   What? Oh no, it's Thursday. I forgot!
MUM   ☐

DIALOGUE 5
TONY   You've spent all morning on the computer, Jill.
JILL   ☐

DIALOGUE 6
CLAIRE   Amanda's really upset with you.
TOMMY   I know. ☐

Adjectives to describe uncomfortable feelings

1 Add the missing vowels to make six words to describe uncomfortable feelings.

1 stck _____   4 wkwrd _____
2 glty _____   5 pzzld _____
3 shmd _____   6 dsprt _____

2 Use the words from Exercise 1 to describe how these people feel.

1 'I don't know why I said that to him. It was a terrible thing to do.' _____

2 'Why would he behave like that? It's not like him at all.'
   _____

3 'I know I shouldn't have but I cheated in the test.'
   _____

4 'It's no good. I really can't see the answer to this equation.' _____

5 'Please help me. Please. I really don't know what to do. I'll do anything …' _____

6 'She's your sister – not your girlfriend? Oh dear. Sorry about that.' _____

Talking about past ability

1 Match the sentence halves.

1 He managed to get the car started and ☐
2 We succeeded in completing the game and ☐
3 She managed to stop the baby crying and ☐
4 He didn't succeed in persuading the police officer and ☐
5 I didn't manage to fix the TV and ☐
6 We didn't succeed in finding a hotel and ☐

a we were able to get to sleep.
b he wasn't able to continue his journey.
c we weren't able to watch the match.
d he was able to continue his journey.
e we weren't able to spend the night there.
f we were able to get to the next level.

2 Compete the sentences with your own ideas about last weekend.

1 I was able to _____ .
2 I succeeded in _____ .
3 I managed to _____ .
4 I wasn't able to _____ .
5 I didn't succeed in _____ .
6 I didn't manage to _____ .

SUMMING UP

1 Complete the dialogue with the missing words. There are four extra words.

light | succeeded | blame | let | puzzled | dear | you made | ashamed | managed | bright | fault

JEN   Hey Tim, how did the match go? Tell me you ¹_____ to get a goal.

TIM   I don't really want to talk about it.

JEN   Oh ²_____ . What happened?

TIM   The only thing I ³_____ in doing was to make a complete fool of myself.

JEN   It can't have been that bad.

TIM   Well it was. I ⁴_____ the whole team down.

JEN   How? What went so wrong?

TIM   The game finished 1 – 1 so there was a penalty shoot-out. I missed the penalty and we lost.

JEN   Poor ⁵_____ .

TIM   I'm so ⁶_____ . It's all my fault.

JEN   Don't be silly. It could have happened to anyone. You can't ⁷_____ yourself.

TIM   Well I do. I'll never be chosen to play again.

JEN   I'm sure you will, but even if you don't, look on the ⁸_____ side. You can hang out with me more.

D BUT IS IT NEWS?
Introducing news

1 Match the statements and responses.

1 Have you heard? ☐
2 Have you heard about Oliver? ☐
3 Did you know Mr Thomas has had an accident? ☐
4 Guess what. ☐
5 You'll never believe what I heard! ☐

a No, what happened?
b So tell me. What did you hear?
c Heard what?
d What?
e No, what's he done now?

2 Write a third line for each mini-dialogue in Exercise 1.

1 _____
2 _____
3 _____
4 _____
5 _____

Ways of speaking

1 What are these people doing? Match the sentences with the verbs in the list.

confessing | introducing | announcing recommending | complaining

1 If you like spicy food, you should try the new Indian restaurant.

_____

2 Ok, it was me who took the money but I was going to put it back, I promise.

_____

3 Why is there never anything good on TV on a Friday night?

_____

4 Olivia, I'd like you to meet Tom.

_____

5 I'd just like to say that Mr Bowden will be leaving the school in April after ten years teaching here.

_____

verb + noun collocations with *make, take, play, do, give*

1 Write the nouns in the list under the correct verb headings. Sometimes there is more than one option.

advantage | advice | a deal | a decision | money
a part | progress | research | revenge | a speech

make	take	play
_____	_____	_____
_____	_____	_____
_____	_____	_____
_____	_____	_____
		_____

do	give
_____	_____
_____	_____
_____	_____
_____	_____

2 Complete the sentences with collocations from Exercise 1.

1 They want an answer tomorrow so we need to _____ soon.

2 The UN _____ an important _____ in ending the conflict.

3 _____ my _____ and don't say anything to him.

4 Scientists are _____ into a cure for the disease.

5 I had to _____ in front of the whole school. I was terrified.

6 They _____ a lot of _____ buying old houses and restoring them. It's a very profitable business.

Cause and effect linkers

1 Complete the sentences with words in the list.

due | because | result | consequently

1 As a _____ of our good behaviour, our teacher has said we can have an end of term party.

2 Not many people knew about the party. _____, not many people turned up.

3 The flights were cancelled _____ of heavy storms.

4 We were late _____ to a massive traffic jam on the motorway.

2 Complete the sentences with your own ideas.

1 I had a really bad headache this morning. Consequently, _____.

2 I couldn't get to sleep last night because of _____.

3 As a result of doing really well in my tests _____.

4 I'm not able to come to your party due to _____.

Sharing news

1 Circle the correct words.

1 If you see Don can you *let / make / allow* him know that the party has been cancelled?

2 I know you'll only be away for a year but you must promise to *get / keep / continue* in touch.

3 I need to *keep / get / make* in touch with Sue. Have you got her number?

4 I'm getting married and I can't wait to *make / take / break* the news to my parents.

5 Miss James asked me to *give / pass / push* on a message that she's going to be five minutes late.

SUMMING UP

1 Put the dialogue in the correct order.

☐	DAD	That's your problem, not mine.
☐	DAD	No, Sue. I'm sorry. There are no more chances. From now on you're on your own in the kitchen.
☐	DAD	Guess what kids. I have made a decision.
1	DAD	Everyone, I'd like to announce something.
☐	DAD	I will. Because of the mess that you always leave in the kitchen I am no longer going to make meals for you.
☐	BILL	I don't really think it's a problem. I quite like the idea of cooking for myself.
☐	BILL	What is it this time, Dad?
☐	SUE	That's not fair, Dad. How are we supposed to eat?
☐	SUE	That's because you don't really care what you eat. But I do. Please Dad. Give us another chance.
☐	SUE	Come on then. Tell us what it is.

1 BROTHERS AND SISTERS

GRAMMAR

Talking about habits SB page 14

1 ★☆☆ **Tick the sentences that refer to habits.**

1 My parents didn't use to take us on holiday. ☐

2 I'm meeting Ken for coffee later. ☐

3 My sister will talk for hours if you let her. ☐

4 I didn't use to watch much TV at all. ☐

5 Charlie tends to leave his homework until the last minute. ☐

6 I can't believe my dad will be 50 next week. ☐

7 My aunt Abi would always get me the most amazing presents for my birthday. ☐

8 My children are always asking me questions. ☐

2 ★★☆ **Look at the sentences again. Do they refer to past, present or future?**

3 ★★☆ **Complete the text with the words/phrases in the list.**

are always trying | would | will always | tends to be
would never | used to keep | always make | used to

I ¹_____ be quite shy when I was younger. There was always a lot of noise at home and I ²_____ just sit quietly in the corner reading a book. It was the same at school. I ³_____ put my hand up when the teacher asked a question. I ⁴_____ quiet and hope she wouldn't pick me.

I'm certainly not shy any more. I can't be. I'm a magician and I provide entertainment at children's parties. It's a lot of fun but it ⁵_____ a little chaotic. The children ⁶_____ to find out how I do my tricks. At the end of my show I ⁷_____ an elephant out of balloons. Of course, all the kids want it but I ⁸_____ give it to the one child who's sat quietly without making too much of a fuss. After all, I know exactly how they feel.

4 ★★☆ **Complete the second sentence so that it has a similar meaning to the first sentence using the word given. Do not change the word. Use between 3 and 6 words, including the word given.**

0 I was quite jealous of my younger brother when I was little.
USED
I _used to be_ quite jealous of my younger brother when I was little.

1 My brother takes my things without asking and it's really annoying.
ALWAYS
My brother is _____ without asking.

2 My mother has a habit of getting our names mixed up.
TENDS
My mother _____ mixed up.

3 Younger children tend to stay in the family home for longer.
WILL
Younger children _____ their parents for longer.

4 I never really got on with my brother when we were kids.
USE
I _____ with my brother when we were kids.

5 My sister and I used to sometimes have fights.
WOULD
My sister and I _____ fights.

5 ★★★ **Complete the sentences so that they are true for you.**

1 I didn't use to _____ when I was little.

2 I tend to _____ when I'm tired.

3 In the school holidays my family would _____ .

4 I will sometimes _____ when I'm hungry.

5 My best friend is always _____ .

Adverbs to express attitude SB page 17

6 ★　　 **Complete the mini-dialogues with the adverbs from the list.**

surely | admittedly | hopefully
annoyingly | honestly

1 A _____ my parents have decided we're not going to Majorca this year.

　B That's a shame. I know you were really looking forward to a bit of Spanish sun.

2 A Are you going to miss your brother when he goes to university next week?

　B _____ I don't think I will and I can't wait to have a bedroom all to myself.

3 A _____ you must be proud of your sister winning the singing competition?

　B I suppose I am. The problem is she won't stop talking about it.

4 A You can't be very happy your brother's taken up the trumpet.

　B Well _____ he'll lose interest in it after a few days.

5 A I can't believe you said that to Lucy.

　B _____ it was a bit mean but sometimes she just really annoys me.

7 ★　　 **Choose the correct options.**

Fri May 1st

[1]*Honestly / Surely / Regrettably* I'm going to win the school art competition, aren't I? I mean my picture's the best by far. [2]*Hopefully / Admittedly / Understandably* the judges will see that and give me first place. [3]*Surely / Obviously / Admittedly* Sue Baker's painting is quite good, but not as good as mine.

Mon May 4th

[4]*Hopefully / Honestly / Regrettably* I didn't get first place in the art competition. I can't quite believe it. [5]*Honestly / Regrettably / Admittedly,* I really thought that prize was mine. [6]*Annoyingly / Understandably / Surely* I'm upset at the moment. [7]*Understandably / Annoyingly / Admittedly* the judges decided that Sue Baker's silly little watercolour painting of a boat was better than my abstract impression of a puddle. [8]*Surely / Hopefully / Obviously* they don't know anything about art.

8 ★★　 **Rewrite the sentences using the adverb form of the underlined words.**

0 The bus was late, which was <u>annoying</u>.
　Annoyingly, the bus was late.

1 I <u>hope</u> I'll get chosen for the school play.
　_____

2 It's <u>obvious</u> that he wasn't happy about what you said.
　_____

3 If I'm <u>honest</u> I don't really care what you do.
　_____

4 They sold all their best players, which was <u>regrettable</u>.
　_____

5 I have to <u>admit</u> that I didn't really try very hard.
　_____

6 It's <u>understandable</u> that they were quite upset about their test results.
　_____

7 I'm <u>sure</u> it won't rain again today.
　_____

GET IT RIGHT!
Adverbs to express attitude

Learners often put adverbs in the wrong position in the sentence.

✓ *Regrettably, I can't come to your party.*
✗ *I ~~regrettably~~ can't come to your party.*

Put the words in order to make correct sentences. Add commas where necessary.

1 get on / my brother and I / hopefully / start / to / better / now / might
　_____

2 new job / regrettably / my / things / just / made / worse
　_____

3 her / doesn't / if / Karen / start / more / respectful / to / teachers / she'll / get / in / honestly / trouble / being
　_____

4 agree / admittedly / don't / on / we / but / still / are / everything / good / we / friends
　_____

5 upset / very / about / you're / behaviour / understandably / inconsiderate / his
　_____

6 were / obviously / use / a / teacher / lazy students / the / not / to / having / such / demanding
　_____

VOCABULARY

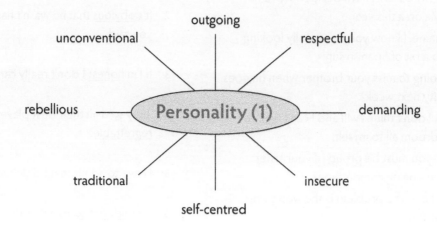

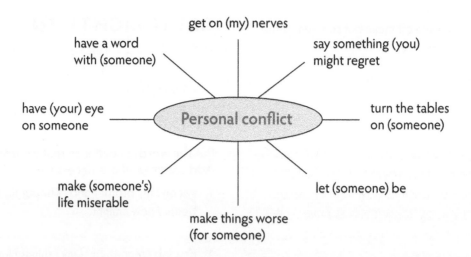

Key words in context

accomplish	I'm 30 and I don't think I've **accomplished** much in my life so far.
burden	Can you carry this for me? Sorry to be a **burden**.
compelling	The new series is **compelling** and I can't wait for the next episode.
diminish	Unfortunately eyesight **diminishes** with age.
era	My gran says the 1960s was a great **era** for pop music and fashion.
genetic	It's thought that autism is **genetic** and passed on through the family.
intense	The pressure on the athletes to win is **intense**.
pester	Stop **pestering** me. Can't you see I'm busy?
regardless (of)	I'm definitely going to the concert **regardless** of how much it costs.
sibling	I've got three **siblings**: a brother and two sisters.

Personality (1) SB page 14

1 ★ Match the adjectives with the pictures.

traditional | insecure | self-centred | respectful
unconventional | rebellious

1 _____

2 _____

3 _____

4 _____

5 _____

6 _____

2 ★★ Match the sentences.

1 My cousin's really outgoing. ☐
2 Don't be so insecure. ☐
3 Larry's very self-centred. ☐
4 I was pretty rebellious as a child. ☐
5 Some of his ideas are quite unconventional. ☐
6 Your friend Adrian's not very respectful. ☐
7 He's a very traditional man. ☐
8 My dad's really demanding. ☐

a In fact the way he treats his parents is quite rude.
b I used to do the exact opposite of what my parents said.
c He wants me home by 10 pm every night!
d He rarely thinks about anyone but himself.
e He will always open a door for a lady.
f You're a wonderful person. You really are.
g We don't always agree, but he's interesting to talk to.
h He loves meeting new people.

3 ★★★ Write a short paragraph about yourself. Choose four of the adjectives in Exercise 2 and say why they apply (or don't apply) to you.

_____

_____

_____

_____

_____

Personal conflict SB page 17

4 ★★ Complete the text with the words in the list.

something | eye | nerves | things
word | life | me | tables

He's been ¹*making my* _____ *miserable* for six months now. At first it wasn't too bad. He was exciting and new but then he soon started to ²*get on my* _____. It was just little things at first, like the noises he would make and always being wherever I was. And now every morning, as soon as I wake up, before I'm even out of bed – 'How are you today?' Why can't he just ³*let* _____ *be*?

I'd ⁴*have a* _____ *with* him about his behaviour but, of course, I can't. And there's no danger of me ⁵*saying* _____ *I might regret* – he doesn't understand a word I say.

To ⁶*make* _____ *worse*, he thinks I actually like him. Or does he? Maybe I'm getting paranoid but I'm beginning to wonder if he's trying to take over my life. Is he trying to ⁷*turn the* _____ *on* me – make me the servant and him the master? I'm going to have to ⁸*keep my* _____ *on* him for sure.

'Your new best friend for life,' that's what it said on the box. Well he isn't and I'm beginning to regret the day I decided to buy myself the RoboFriend 200X.

5 ★★ Match the expressions in italics in Exercise 4 with the definitions.

1 being really unkind to someone over a long period of time ☐
2 have a serious talk with someone about something you're not happy about ☐
3 increase a bad situation ☐
4 really annoy someone ☐
5 watch someone carefully either to protect them or to make sure they behave well ☐
6 express something bad out of anger or frustration ☐
7 leave someone alone and not bother them ☐
8 reverse a situation ☐

READING

1 **REMEMBER AND CHECK** Complete the sentences with *only, eldest, second, middle* or *youngest*. Then read the article on page 13 of the Student's Book again and check.

According to the text...

1 _____ children don't do as well as they could do.

2 _____ children often don't do things the expected way.

3 _____ children might feel they never live up to expectations.

4 _____ children might be inspired to do better than their siblings.

5 _____ children are often confused about where they belong in the family.

6 _____ children want to try and please their parents.

7 _____ children are most like their parents.

8 _____ children tend to think mainly of themselves.

2 Read the true story. How are Anaïs and Samantha related?

LONG-LOST ...

One day in December 2012 Anaïs Bordier, a French student studying fashion in London, was surprised to see that another student had posted a video of her on her Facebook page. Anaïs was intrigued because she had never made a video of herself. When she watched the video the mystery deepened. The girl in the video looked exactly like her but it was not her. Unfortunately as there was no name on the video there was no way of investigating any further.

About a month later Anaïs came across another video of the same girl. It was a trailer for a film. Suddenly she had a lead. She investigated and found from the cast list that the girl's name was Samantha Futerman. She was an actress in the US. She also found out that they shared the same birthday. But even more surprising, Samantha, like herself, had been born in South Korea.

Anaïs had always known that she was adopted. She knew she had been born in the city of Busan in South Korea, the only child of a young, unmarried woman. She had been adopted by a French couple and had spent her life in France. But now she was starting to question

whether or not she knew the whole truth. She phoned her mother who asked the question she had secretly been asking herself; could she have a twin?

Anaïs decided to get in touch with Samantha and sent her a message. She told Samantha to check out her Facebook page. When Samantha got back in touch she sent a copy of her adoption certificate. They had been born in the same hospital. It was official. They were twins!

They exchanged photos and arranged to speak on Skype. Anaïs was amazed. They had the same laugh, the same facial movements. They even had similar haircuts. They spoke for three hours.

Eventually the girls decided to meet. Samantha, accompanied by her parents and brothers, flew over to London. Anaïs took her mother and a few friends along to the meeting for moral support. But there was no need. As soon as they came face-to-face the girls knew they wanted to be alone and catch up on all the missing years. So they went off to have lunch, stopping all the way to check out their reflections in shop windows to make sure it wasn't all just a dream.

Later that day, the girls received more news; they weren't just twins, they were also identical twins.

Anaïs still wonders why they were separated at birth. Samantha said that she had once tried to make contact with their birth mother but the woman named on the adoption papers had told her she had the wrong person. But for Anaïs none of this matters anymore. She has found a sister who she didn't even know existed, and although they live on different continents, they spend as much time as they possibly can together.

3 Read the story again and put the events in the order which they happened.

☐ Anaïs finds out information about the mystery girl.

☐ Anaïs and her mother wonder if she could have a twin.

☐ The girls get together.

☐ Anaïs makes contact with Samantha.

☐ Anaïs watches a video of someone who looks just like her.

☐ Anaïs gets confirmation she's a twin.

☐ Anaïs learns that she is adopted.

☐ The girls find out exactly how they are related.

4 Imagine Samantha and Anaïs' first Skype call and write a short dialogue.

DEVELOPING WRITING

A personal email

1 Read the email and answer the questions.

1 What is Lola's big news?

_____

2 Who is Jennie?

_____

3 Why does she admire her so much?

_____

2 Read through the first paragraph again. Which of these things does Lola do?

- [ ] refers to her friend's suggestion
- [ ] gives reasons for the delay in her reply
- [ ] tells her friend what's been happening in her life
- [ ] responds to her friend's news
- [ ] enquires how her friend is

3 Read through the email again and complete Lola's notes.

Family hero: _____
(my _____)
Jennie's challenge: living with
_____
What Jennie wants: _____
Examples of how she does this:
_____

4 Imagine you are Steph. You have decided to enter the competition. Write to Lola and tell her who you have chosen and why. Write 220–260 words. Don't forget to respond to her letter first and answer her questions.

CHECKLIST ✓

_____
_____
_____
_____
_____

To   steph99@mymail.com
Subject   My big news!

Hi Steph,

How are you? Hope all is well. So sorry I haven't written for a while but I've been pretty busy with school work. Anyway, thanks for your invitation to visit this summer. I've had a word with Mum and Dad and they said they'll think about it. I'll let you know as soon as they make their minds up.

So my big news is that I've entered a national essay writing competition. It's being run by The Daily Telegraph and they want readers to nominate a family hero. You just have to choose a relative and answer why they deserve to win an award. It was really easy for me because Jennie, my older sister, has always been my hero. I think I told you she has autism, which means life can be pretty tough for her at times. However, when she isn't trying to find ways of being able to cope better with her everyday challenges, she's working to help others understand more about the condition. For example, she spoke for 20 minutes in a school assembly last week about what it's like to be autistic. It wasn't an easy thing for her to do but it was amazing to see the reaction of the other students. I was so proud of her. I've attached a photo of her in the assembly. She also spends most of her weekends working with a charity that offers support to children who have autistic siblings (like me). I don't suppose I'll win but it felt good just to sit down and put into writing just how amazing Jennie is.

I promise I'll let you know if I do win though. Actually the closing date for entries is the 30th, I believe, so if you want to write in about anyone, you've still got time. Let me know if you do decide to enter.

Love,
Lola

LISTENING

1 🔊04 **Listen to Connie talking with her siblings. For each sibling circle the word Connie might use to describe them.**

Jasmine

Frank

Lucy

1 Jasmine: *insecure / traditional / self-centred*

2 Frank: *rebellious / outgoing / respectful*

3 Lucy: *self-centred / unconventional / insecure*

2 🔊04 **Listen again and mark the sentences T (true), F (false) or DS (doesn't say).**

Conversation 1

1 Jasmine feels guilty for drinking her sister's coke. ☐

2 Connie is angry because she had a bad day at school. ☐

Conversation 2

3 Connie thinks Frank's piercing looks cool. ☐

4 Connie's got pierced ears. ☐

Conversation 3

5 Lucy had an argument with her best friend. ☐

6 Connie is shocked by the behaviour of some of her sister's friends. ☐

3 **Look at the lines from the conversations. What technique is being used to add emphasis? Look on page 15 of the Student's Book to help you.**

1 You've drunk my coke, haven't you? _____

2 Since when has Mum ever bought us coke? _____

3 You do get on my nerves sometimes. _____

4 Tell me, have you gone completely mad? _____

5 You do know what they think about piercings, don't you? _____

6 You must be joking. Make-up! But you're not even 12 yet. _____

7 All your friends, Lucy? You're telling me that all your friends wear make-up? _____

DIALOGUE

1 **Put the dialogue in order.**

☐ CONNIE What do you mean? Why would I want to go there?

☐ CONNIE You know exactly what; my hairbrush. What have you done with it?

☐ CONNIE I will and if I find it, there will be trouble.

☐ CONNIE I'm sorry but I don't believe you. You're always taking my things without asking.

☐ CONNIE So you won't mind if I take a look in your room then, will you?

☐1 CONNIE Ok, Jasmine, where is it?

☐ JASMINE No, I won't. Go ahead. Be my guest.

☐ JASMINE Where's what?

☐ JASMINE Well this time I'm not guilty. Sorry to disappoint you.

☐ JASMINE But before you waste your time, you might want to check in Lucy's room first.

☐ JASMINE Nothing. I've done nothing with your stupid hairbrush.

☐ JASMINE Just that maybe your favourite baby sister has something that belongs to you. I'm not always the problem, you know.

2 **Choose one of the following and write a ten line dialogue. Use at least three examples of emphatic language.**

a Connie goes into Lucy's bedroom and finds Lucy using her hairbrush.

b Frank's dad notices his pierced tongue.

Pronunciation

Intonation: showing emotions
Go to page 118. 🔊

CAMBRIDGE ENGLISH: Advanced

Reading and Use of English Part 2

1 For questions 1–8, read the text below and think of the word which best fits each gap. Use only one word in each gap. There is an example at the beginning (0).

Cousins

What ⁰ _is_ it about cousins that makes them so special?
I remember when I was a kid we ¹_____ to hang out with
our cousins every summer holiday. They really were great times.
Now I watch the joy that my ²_____ children experience
every time we go and visit my sister and her children.
³_____ five days I hardly see my three boys as they're off
exploring and playing with a brand ⁴_____ set of toys.
But what's even more amazing is that I hardly hear them either.
Back home I'm called upon at ⁵_____ three times a day to break up a fight between two of them but when
they're with their cousins it's as if they've all suddenly become the best ⁶_____ friends. There's no arguing.
No one seems to get on anyone else's nerves. And I rarely have to have words with any of them. There are
often a few tears in the back of the car when we have to leave and promises that we ⁷_____ be back to
visit soon. Ten minutes later as I'm pulling onto the motorway the fighting begins. It's amazing ⁸_____
quickly normal service is resumed.

2 For questions 1–8, read the text below and think of the word which best fits each gap. Use only one word in each gap. There is an example at the beginning (0).

ANIMAL FAMILIES

Family relationships play ⁰ _such_ an important part in the human
world, from shaping our individual personalities to providing
inspiration for much of our storytelling. Psychologists have
dedicated their lives to the subject and hundreds of books have
¹_____ written on the topic. However, when it comes to the
animal kingdom, not nearly as ²_____ research has been
done. In his book *Sisters and Brothers: Sibling Relationships in the
Animal World*, author Steve Jenkins takes a look ³_____ some
of the more interesting examples of sibling behaviour in different
species of animals. Perhaps ⁴_____ of the biggest differences is that while multiple births are rare in humans,
they are commonplace for many animals. It ⁵_____ be quite unusual for a cat to give birth to only one kitten.
As a consequence, a lot of newly born animals find they are part of a large family ⁶_____ the day they are born.
This can often lead to quite cruel consequences with weaker siblings dying from ⁷_____ unable to fight for the
food that they need. ⁸_____ some extreme cases they can be deliberately killed by a brother or sister.

2 | SLEEP ON IT

GRAMMAR

Past tenses with hypothetical meaning SB page 22

1 ★☆☆ **Circle the correct option.**

1 It's time we *stop / stopped* talking and did something about it.

2 Mum wishes she *doesn't / didn't* have so much work to do.

3 I'd prefer *to text / text* him rather than give him a call.

4 If only our house *was / is* a bit bigger. I'd love to have my own bedroom.

5 I'd prefer he *say / said* sorry in person.

6 It's time *turn / to turn* off your computer and do something else.

7 I wish I *knew / know* the answer to that question. I really wish I *do / did*.

8 If only I *have / had* enough money to buy a new tablet.

2 ★★☆ **Complete the sentences with the correct form of the verb in brackets.**

1 It's time you _____ to bed. You can't stop yawning. (go)

2 I wish this bed _____ so hard. It's really uncomfortable. (not be)

3 If only I _____ some sleeping tablets. They would help me get to sleep. (have)

4 I'd prefer it if you _____ talking. I'm trying to get to sleep. (stop)

5 If only the neighbours _____ their music so loud. I can't get to sleep. (not play)

6 I wish I _____ stop thinking about my exam tomorrow. (can)

7 It's time we _____ a new bed. This one's about to collapse. (buy)

8 I'd prefer it if we _____ the light on. It's stopping me from getting to sleep. (not keep)

3 ★★☆ **Rewrite the sentences using the word in brackets.**

0 You need to get up now. (time)
   It's time you got up now.

1 It would be nice to live in the countryside. (wish)
   _____

2 I think we should leave half an hour earlier. (prefer)
   _____

3 It's 2 pm and I haven't had lunch yet. That's why I'm so hungry! (time)
   _____

4 I'd like it to stop raining now! (only)
   _____

5 My choice would be to take a taxi. (prefer)
   _____

4 ★★★ **Complete the sentences with your own ideas.**

I'd prefer to _____

I wish _____

If only _____

It's time _____

Adverbs for modifying comparatives
SB page 25

5 ★   Complete the dialogue with the phrases in the list. There are three you won't use.

considerably quicker | far more | a lot | more complex
far bigger | it's way | be much | lot more

TIM   So tell me about this book idea of yours. It's a kind of dream dictionary, isn't it?

JO   No, it's [1]_____ exciting than that. Think of it as a dream encyclopedia.

TIM   So you use it to find out what your dream might mean.

JO   No, it's [2]_____ more useful than that. Yes, you can find out about your dream but it also gives you advice on how to act on this information.

TIM   So I dream about a cat and then I look up 'cat' in your book and it tells me what my dream means and what to do about it?

JO   No, it's considerably [3]_____ than that. You'll need to look at the context of your dream too.

TIM   But how are you going to fit all of this in a book?

JO   It's going to be [4]_____ than just a book. It's going to be a series of twenty books.

TIM   Twenty! And you're going to write all this in a year?

JO   A year? No, it's going to be [5]_____ than that. I hope to have it finished by May.

TIM   But we're already in March!

6 ★★   Rewrite the sentences including the word in brackets to modify the comparative. Sometimes this will change the meaning of the sentence.

1   He is as talented as his younger brother. (nowhere near)

_____

2   The Eiffel Tower is taller than I thought it would be. (far)

_____

3   It is cheaper to take the bus than the train. (way)

_____

4   That rollercoaster is as scary as it looks. (nothing like)

_____

5   This exam is more difficult than the one you did last week. (significantly)

_____

6   This situation is more serious than we first thought. (drastically)

_____

7 ★★★ Complete the sentences with your own ideas.

1   _____ is far more exciting than I thought it would be.

2   _____ is notably more difficult than when my parents were young.

3   _____ is significantly more interesting than playing computer games.

4   _____ is way easier than my teacher said it would be.

5   _____ is much more enjoyable than watching TV.

6   _____ is nowhere near as boring as _____.

7   _____ is not nearly as complicated as _____.

8   _____ is a lot more disgusting than _____.

GET IT RIGHT!

as ... as ...

Learners often omit *as* in *as ... as* phrases when using modifiers.

✓ *Bill is nowhere near **as** clever a builder **as** Bob.*

✗ *Bill is nowhere near clever a builder as Bob.*

Rewrite the following sentences with *as ... as* using *not nearly*, *nowhere near* or *nothing like*.

0   I'm surprised but you are much more surprised than me.

I'm not nearly as surprised as you. /
I'm nowhere near as surprised as you. /
I'm nothing like as surprised as you.

1   My dream was strange but yours was far stranger!

_____

2   Some countries don't value the importance of sleep while other nations value it much more.

_____

3   Working in this office isn't very interesting. My dream job is much more interesting.

_____

4   Brazilians take naps far more than the Japanese.

_____

5   Dream incorporation is much less mysterious than it seems.

_____

VOCABULARY

Sleep

nod off
fall asleep
lie in
a light sleeper
fast asleep
snore loudly
under the covers
take a nap

a lack of sleep
oversleep
skip sleep
get enough sleep
get 7 hours' sleep

Idioms with *sleep* and *dream*

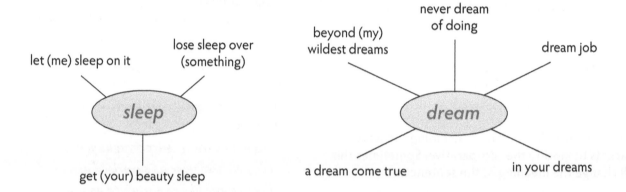

let (me) sleep on it

lose sleep over (something)

sleep

get (your) beauty sleep

never dream of doing

beyond (my) wildest dreams

dream job

dream

a dream come true

in your dreams

Key words in context

cast	The **cast** of this film is unknown. I've never heard of any of the actors.
disquieting	There might be a war between the two countries – it's very **disquieting** for the people who live there.
exaggerated	I think saying that this is the worst day of your life is a bit **exaggerated**, isn't it?
head start	I'll give you a five-minute **head start** but I'll still get home before you.
immune system	The doctors say my **immune system** is weak and I'm likely to catch viruses more easily.
invade	The war started when one country decided to **invade** the other.
limb	I know he broke a **limb**. I think it was his right arm, or was it his leg?
optimum	I think 32 is the **optimum** age for getting married.
paralysed	He was **paralysed** from the neck down after the accident.
prone	I'm **prone** to getting headaches if I stay out in the sun too long.
surge	As soon as the doors opened all the fans **surged** towards the stage.
trigger	The government's decision to stop free healthcare **triggered** protests all over the country.

Sleep `SB page 22`

1 ★ Match the phrases with the definitions.

1 take a nap ☐
2 lie in ☐
3 a light sleeper ☐
4 fast asleep ☐
5 snore loudly ☐
6 nod off ☐
7 fall asleep ☐
8 under the covers ☐

a to stay in bed later than usual in the morning
b someone who is easily woken up
c to breathe in a very noisy way while you are sleeping
d to start to sleep
e to begin sleeping, especially not intentionally
f in bed, under the bed sheets
g have a short sleep, especially during the day
h sleeping deeply

2 ★★ Complete the text with the phrases from Exercise 1.

I like sleeping. You might say it's one of my hobbies. At bedtime I always ^{1}_____ really easily. I like to get at least eight hours a night if I can and sometimes I'll ^{2}_____ in the afternoon. I've also been known to ^{3}_____ on the school bus on the way home. That can be a bit embarrassing.
I'm not really a big fan of early mornings. That's why I like the weekends so much when you have a chance to ^{4}_____ (if Mum and Dad let me, that is). During the week I have to get up at 7 am, which is really hard and sometimes my parents have to practically pull me out from ^{5}_____ to get me out of bed.
I share a bedroom with my twin sister. She likes her sleep too and sometimes she ^{6}_____ really _____. Luckily I'm not a ^{7}_____ so I don't really hear her. I'm usually ^{8}_____ by the time she goes to bed anyway!

3 ★★ Choose the correct options.

1 I sometimes forget to set my alarm and *lie in / oversleep* in the mornings.
2 My brother doesn't get *full / enough* sleep – he plays computer games all night!
3 I think it's really bad to *skip / lack* sleep when studying for exams.
4 She's suffering from a *lack / need* of sleep.
5 I like to try and *get / find* 8 hours' sleep a night.

4 ★★★ Write a short paragraph about your sleeping habits. Write about:

● how much you sleep
● where you sleep
● weekday mornings vs. weekend mornings

Idioms with *sleep* and *dream* `SB page 25`

5 ★★ Put the words in order to make phrases.

1 dreams / my / it's / wildest / beyond

_____

2 something / dream / that / of / I'd / doing / never / like _____
3 a / true / come / dream / it's _____
4 my / to / get / need / sleep / beauty / I _____

5 sleep / it / lose / over / don't _____
6 dreams / your / in _____
7 me / it / on / sleep / let _____
8 my / dream / it's / job _____

6 ★★ Use the phrases in Exercise 5 to complete the replies in the mini-dialogues. Sometimes more than one may be possible.

1 A So how do you feel about being chosen to be the new James Bond?
  B _____
2 A Tommy, you didn't eat my chocolate bar that was in the fridge, did you?
  B Me? _____
3 A I'm a bit worried about my driving test tomorrow.
  B Well _____. I'm sure you'll be fine.
4 A What – you're off to bed already? It's only 9 o'clock.
  B I know but _____
5 A So what do you say? Shall we go camping this weekend?
  B I'm not sure. _____ and I'll give you an answer in the morning.
6 A Do you think Michelle Saunders would go to the cinema with me?
  B _____
7 A So, what's it like being a pilot?
  B _____. It's perfect.
8 A How does it feel being reunited with your long lost twin sister?
  B _____. Something I thought would never happen.

READING

1 REMEMBER AND CHECK **Answer the questions. Then read the article on page 21 of the Student's Book again and check.**

1 Why are the results from a recent survey into teenage sleeping habits worrying?

2 What effects of a lack of sleep are being seen in schools?

3 What physical and mental health problems can a lack of sleep cause?

4 Why can teenagers be excused for their 'anti-social' sleeping habits?

5 What decision could be taken by the authorities to help address the problem?

6 How can teenagers be encouraged to tackle the problem on a personal level?

2 Read the article and choose the best title for it.

A Good sleeping habits   **B** The night-time secrets of success   **C** Achieve more with a good night's sleep

---

It's no secret that getting a good night's sleep is an important part of leading a healthy lifestyle. Of course, not everyone needs the same amount of sleep but what is generally agreed on is that the quality rather than quantity of your sleep time can have a huge influence on your wellbeing during the day. And, as many doctors agree, one way of ensuring that quality is to look closely at your pre-sleep routine. We can look to some of the world's most important people as examples of how to go about doing this.

The American inventor and politician Benjamin Franklin liked to ask himself the same question just before going to sleep; 'What good have I done today?' In his autobiography he wrote that by answering this question at the end of each day, he hoped to achieve 'moral perfection'. He also listed other routines such as putting things in order, having supper, listening to music or chatting.

Of course, it's not always so easy to find time to relax in the evenings when you're in charge of one of the world's largest economies. Former US president Barack Obama has referred to himself as a night owl and would often still be discussing business with his staff until 11 pm, although he would always try and have dinner with his family and put his children to bed before getting back to work.

Many of today's top business people have also described their night-time habits. Sheryl Sandberg is the chief operating officer for Facebook. Even though she works in an industry in which communication is vital, she realises the importance of having time to yourself and makes sure her phone is switched off at night to avoid being woken up, although she admits this can be tricky.

In the world of computing, you won't find a bigger name than Bill Gates. The co-founder of Microsoft and one of the world's richest men has described how he likes to put aside around an hour each night before he goes to bed to read. He particularly enjoys biographies, history books and magazines such as *The Economist* and *Scientific America*. He finds the practice helps him get to sleep although he does admit that a really good book can keep him up much later. He also strongly recommends getting a good seven hours' sleep, though he admits it's not always possible to do so.

When it comes to how long you sleep, it'll be hard to find anyone to beat Mariah Carey. The pop sensation has said that she likes to get around 15 hours a night. That's nearly two thirds of the day! Mariah says that she needs this much to ensure she can hit those incredible high notes she's so famous for.

But perhaps the person with the most particular routine is the horror writer Stephen King. He explains that his pillows have to be lined up in a certain way with the open side pointing to the other side of the bed. He admits that he has no idea why things have to be this way. However, having sold more than 350 million books in his career, why mess with a winning formula?

---

3 Read the article again and answer the questions with the surname of the person (sometimes there is more than one possibility):

Who:

1 sometimes goes to sleep later than they intended to? _____

2 does something they find difficult to do? _____

3 likes the bed to be arranged in a particular way? _____

4 liked to analyse what they had done during the day? _____

5 made sure their evenings was not all work? _____

6 claims good sleep is needed to help them in their profession? _____

4 Write a short paragraph about what you do before you go to bed each night.

DEVELOPING WRITING

A proposal

1 Read the proposal and answer the questions.

What is the difference between a duvet day and a …

a sick day? _____

b holiday? _____

Subject: A proposal to introduce 'duvet days' to the company

The principal aim of this proposal is to evaluate the effect sick days have on our company and to recommend the introduction of 'duvet days' to help the situation.

According to a recent report the average UK worker takes 9.1 sick days a year, and these unscheduled breaks are costing the UK economy around £29 billion per annum. Furthermore, it shows that in around 12% of these cases the illnesses aren't genuine.

In an ever-changing working environment, people are spending longer at work. This is leading to cases of stress which in turn are causing our staff to take more and more sick days.

In a number of companies, 'duvet days' have been introduced to help combat this problem. In brief, a duvet day is an officially endorsed day when a worker can choose not to come into work for reasons which they do not need to specify. Unlike holiday entitlement, employees do not have to prearrange these days.

We firmly believe that by allocating our employees a number of duvet days each year, we will allow them to manage their own time more effectively and avoid the complications caused by overworking. They will still be expected to meet their deadlines on time but duvet days will offer them more freedom in achieving this.

We strongly recommend that the company conduct a trial run of offering duvet days. We suggest that the effects of this on the company should be monitored and if these are shown to be beneficial, duvet days should be made part of company policy soon.

Writing tip: a proposal

Proposals are similar to reports in that both writing genres aim to give information about a situation. However, proposals also make recommendations for future action.

- Start your proposal by saying what it is about.
- You should then outline the background information, using statistical evidence if relevant.
- The next paragraph should detail your ideas on what should be done to improve this situation, pointing out all the benefits from the proposed course of action.
- Finally, a short paragraph is needed to emphasise why you feel your proposal should be adopted.

2 Complete the examples of useful language with the phrases used in the proposal.

Ways of introducing the reason for the proposal
- The main purpose …
- The prime objective of …
- The intention of …
- 1 _____

Introducing statistical information
- The results of a recent survey suggest …
- A scientific study has shown …
- The findings of the latest opinion polls are …
- 2 _____

Ways of putting across your opinion
- It is our belief …   3 _____
- In our opinion …   4 _____

3 You want to introduce duvet days to your school. Add two more points to each list.

Benefits
- It will allow students to recover from illnesses.
- _____
- _____

Points to consider
- How will students catch up on work they miss?
- _____
- _____

4 Write a proposal recommending duvet days for students at your school. Write 220–260 words.

CHECKLIST ✓

LISTENING

1 🔊 06 **Listen to the conversations. What's keeping these people up at night? Write the names** *Bobby*, *Jackie* **or** *Olivia* **under the pictures. There is one extra picture.**

1 _____ 2 _____ 3 _____ 4 _____

2 🔊 06 **Listen again and mark the sentences T (true) or F (false).**

Conversation 1

1 The police didn't do anything about Bobby's complaint. ☐

2 Bobby has decided that earplugs are his last chance of getting a good night's sleep. ☐

Conversation 2

3 Jackie's had problems with dogs barking in the past. ☐

4 Jackie thinks her house might be haunted. ☐

Conversation 3

5 Olivia's brother has had a snoring problem for a few years. ☐

6 Megan defends Olivia's brother. ☐

3 🔊 06 **Complete the advice with the missing suggestions. Then listen again and check.**

Conversation 1

1 Well, you might want to consider

_____

Conversation 2

2 I recommend _____ to come and have a look.

Conversation 3

3 Well try not to

_____

4 I find that _____ is a good way of falling asleep.

DIALOGUE

1 **Complete the dialogue with the missing lines.**

LINDA Hi Dave. How's the house going?

DAVE ☐

LINDA Four weeks!

DAVE ☐

LINDA Well, try not to think about it too much. It'll look wonderful when it's finished.

DAVE ☐

LINDA And while you're waiting, the insurance company's paying for a hotel, right? How is it by the way?

DAVE ☐

LINDA You might want to consider talking to the manager. Four weeks is a long time to be sleeping on an uncomfortable bed.

DAVE ☐

LINDA I recommend getting your own pillows from your house.

DAVE ☐

1 That's not a bad idea. I could ask him to change the pillows too.

2 It's OK, nothing special. The bed's a bit uncomfortable though.

3 I certainly hope it will.

4 The builders say they'll need another four weeks.

5 I might just do that. They're one of the few things that didn't get ruined by the flood.

6 Yes, the water did a lot of damage.

2 **Write a dialogue of about 10 lines between someone who has a sleeping problem and a friend who is trying to give them some advice.**

Pronunciation

Different ways of pronouncing *c* and *g*

Go to page 118. 🔊

Reading and Use of English Part 1

Exam guide: multiple-choice cloze

Part 1 of the Advanced Reading and Use of English exam is designed to test your knowledge of vocabulary. Unlike Part 2 (the open cloze) you will not be tested on grammatical structures. Areas of vocabulary that commonly feature include: idiomatic language including phrasal verbs, fixed phrases, words with similar meaning and collocations.

- Look carefully at the meaning of the sentence which the words are in. Sometimes you will also need to consider the sentence after. Make sure that the word you choose makes sense in the sentence.
- Look carefully at the words immediately before and after the gap. These will give you clues as to whether the word is part of a fixed phrase.
- Finally, if you have time, read through the whole passage again with your choices in place. Does the text make sense with the words that you have chosen?

1 For questions 1–8, read the text below and decide which answer (A, B, C or D) best fits each gap. There is an example at the beginning (0).

A cure for snoring

I'm what you might describe as a (0) _____ sleeper. I'll wake up at the slightest noise and usually find it difficult to get back to sleep. (1) _____ I rarely get a good night's sleep, meaning I'm often moody and irritable throughout the day. I've also been known to nod (2) _____ at my desk, much to the amusement of my colleagues. More often than not, it is my husband's snoring that (3) _____ my sleeplessness. Although I'm usually fast asleep when he comes to bed, it's never long before his snoring (4) _____ my sleep and I'm wide awake not long after.

Therefore, when I read about a miracle cure for people who snore promising a 100% success guarantee it was something (5) _____ my wildest dreams. My husband was a little unsure, but then he denies that he has a problem in the first place. The treatment involves the insertion of a small appliance that sits between your teeth and (6) _____ a blockage of the soft tissue at the back of your throat, which is what causes the snoring. It's simple, easy to fit and not (7) _____ expensive. That final consideration is what has led my husband to reluctantly agree to (8) _____ it a go. Hopefully, this time next week my sleeping problem will have been solved.

0	A weak	B light	C heavy	D fragile
1	A Contrary	B Resultantly	C Consequently	D However
2	A off	B through	C over	D out
3	A begins	B makes	C triggers	D generates
4	A intrudes	B interferes	C interrupts	D infects
5	A further	B afar	C outside	D beyond
6	A avoids	B prevents	C causes	D cleans
7	A offensively	B shamefully	C outrageously	D disgracefully
8	A try	B have	C offer	D give

CONSOLIDATION

LISTENING

1 🔊08 Listen to Lydia talking to Paul about being the eldest child. Which of these complaints does she have?

- [ ] She can never do well enough at school for her parents.
- [ ] Her parents expect her to help out in the house too much.
- [ ] Her parents give her younger sister more freedom.
- [ ] Her parents expect her to act more maturely.
- [ ] She's not allowed to go to parties.
- [ ] Her parents think she treats her younger sister badly.

2 🔊08 Listen again and decide if the sentences are T (true), F (false) or DS (doesn't say).

1 Lydia's favourite subject at school is PE.
2 Lydia feels that her parents have forgotten what it's like to be young.
3 Lydia wants her parents to tell her that they're proud of her.
4 Lauren is two years younger than Lydia.
5 Lydia's parents accuse her of not doing what is expected.
6 Paul doesn't really sympathise with Lydia.
7 Paul is one of three brothers.
8 Paul often sticks up for his brother.

GRAMMAR

3 Rewrite or correct the sentences to include the word in brackets.

1 I don't know why I said that. (honestly)
_____

2 If we didn't have to go to school today. (only)
_____

3 That was the worst game of football ever played. (surely)
_____

4 It's quicker to walk there than to take the car. (far)
_____

5 My brother is trying to get me in trouble. (always)
_____

6 I'd prefer take a break and finish this tomorrow. (to)
_____

7 The test was nowhere as difficult as I thought it would be. (near)
_____

8 We used be friends until he started going out with my sister. (to)
_____

VOCABULARY

4 Match the sentence halves.

1 If you're feeling tired,　　　　　　[ ]
2 If you don't need to get up early tomorrow,　　[ ]
3 If your brother snores so loudly,　　[ ]
4 If you're a light sleeper,　　　　　[ ]
5 If she's getting on your nerves,　　[ ]
6 If you're getting bullied at school,　[ ]
7 If she's already said sorry,　　　　[ ]
8 If you're scared of making things worse,　　[ ]

a why don't you sleep in a different room?
b why don't you avoid her for a while?
c why don't you just let her be?
d why don't you lie in?
e then don't say anything to her.
f why don't you have a word with your teacher?
g why don't you take a quick nap before dinner?
h why don't you wear earplugs?

5 Choose from the words in the list to describe these people.

traditional | rebellious | demanding
self-centred | outgoing | insecure

1 'I love travelling by bus. There's always someone new to talk to.'
_____

2 'I don't care what Dad says. I'm going to that party tonight.'
_____

3 'I'm not having a birthday party in case no one comes.'
_____

4 'The audience is obviously here just to see me.'
_____

5 'I believe that a man should always open a door for a lady.'
_____

6 'Get me a glass of water – now!'
_____

DIALOGUE

6 Complete the dialogue with the phrases in the list. There are two you won't use.

light | always taking | rebellious | did you
self-centred | tell me | consider getting
didn't you

ALICE   ¹_____ you haven't taken my alarm clock again.

JODY   My phone stopped working, and I need to get up really early tomorrow.

ALICE   So you thought you could just take mine, ²_____?

JODY   Well, you never use it. You're a really ³_____ sleeper.

ALICE   That's not the point. It's mine and you should ask. You're ⁴_____ my things without asking.

JODY   Someone's in a bad mood today. You might want to ⁵_____ a bit more sleep.

ALICE   Actually I'm not. I'm just tired of you being so ⁶_____.

READING

7 Read the article and answer the questions.

1 Why does the writer believe people should care more about their beds?

_____

2 What gadgets does the Jado Steel Gold Bed have?

_____

3 How much more expensive is the floating bed than the Jado Steel Gold Bed?

_____

4 How does the floating bed work?

_____

5 How is the royal bed described?

_____

6 In what circumstances was it discovered?

_____

WRITING

8 Think about your perfect bed and write a paragraph to describe it. Write about 200–220 words. Include:

- what the bed is made of
- what features it would have

Amazing beds

Considering we spend around a third of our lives in or on our beds, they should be the most important item of furniture in the home. Yet with the average bed costing around £500, most people are happy to spend more on their home entertainment system than they are on their bed. I decided to take a look at what you could get if you decided to pay a bit more.

For example, with around £440,000 you could get yourself a Jado Steel Gold Bed. This bed comes with all the luxury you would expect at such a price tag. It is coated in gold and has Swarovski crystals embedded into the headboard. But what really makes this a teenage dream bed are the 'extras' that are included: a PlayStation games console, a BOSE sound system, Blu-ray player and plasma TV screen that folds away when you finally decide to get some sleep. Oh, did I forget to mention that the TV is also coated in gold?

If you'd prefer to spend your extra cash on technological innovation (rather than a whole load of gadgets) then can I suggest the magnetic floating bed? It will cost you quite a bit more (just over £1 million in total) but your bed will certainly be the talking point of your home. Designed by Dutch architect Janjaap Ruijssenaars and taking more than six years to develop, this bed refuses to obey the laws of gravity as it floats just under half a metre above the floor. It uses an amazingly strong magnetic field to do so, which I presume doesn't affect your sleep.

But for the ultimate bedroom showpiece, how about one that is nearly 500 years old and was once slept in by British royalty? This solid oak, four poster bed with elegant carvings belonged to King Henry VII and his wife Elizabeth of York. It was only discovered a few years ago when a team of builders came across it while renovating a small hotel in Chester. They left it outside in the yard where it remained for days until a man from a local auction house came to pick it up. The bed was then bought at auction by Ian Coulson, a collector and four poster bed expert. He paid £2,100 and then set about finding out more about his new bed. After extensive DNA testing it was confirmed to have belonged to the king. So what would this one-of-a-kind royal bed now cost you? Around £20 million!

3 LUCKY BREAKS

GRAMMAR
Mixed conditionals (review) SB page 32

1 ★☆☆ **Match the sentence halves.**

1 If Kathy were a more careful driver ☐
2 I'd be at home by now ☐
3 Jeremy wouldn't be embarrassed ☐
4 If I hadn't watched the news last night ☐
5 If Mayumi hadn't gone to the beach in Rio ☐
6 Theresa would probably be acting in the theatre now ☐
7 We wouldn't be so unhappy now ☐
8 If Peter paid more attention ☐

a I wouldn't know about the plane crash.
b she wouldn't be married to a Brazilian.
c if I hadn't missed the last bus.
d if she hadn't been late for that audition.
e if we hadn't lost that last match.
f she wouldn't have had that accident.
g he wouldn't have missed the turning and got lost.
h if he hadn't tripped and fallen over on the dance floor.

2 ★★☆ **Complete the gaps with** were / weren't, would / wouldn't **and** had / hadn't.

1 Sally _____ be a top gymnast if she _____ started training very young. She was only four when she began.
2 If Mike _____ read the news, he _____ know the buses were on strike and he _____ be standing waiting at the bus stop at the moment.
3 Sue finds learning French difficult. If she _____ been born in France, she _____ need to study French now.
4 If he _____ better at science, Ken _____ have won the quiz show.
5 Monica _____ have a bandage on her foot if she _____ tripped over the cat and broken her ankle.
6 Denny is 2.1 m tall. If Denny _____ over 2 metres tall, he _____ have started to play basketball.
7 Miranda _____ have been able to reach the top shelf if she _____ taller.
8 Jacqueline _____ be so nervous about the exam if she _____ paid more attention in class.

3 ★★☆ **Complete the sentences with the correct form of the verbs in brackets.**

1 If I _____ (not spend) so much money on that computer last month, I _____ (be) in Spain on holiday now.
2 I _____ (not be) hungry now if my friends _____ (wake) me up in time for breakfast.
3 If my dad _____ (be) younger, he _____ (go) to the rock concert last night.
4 I _____ (not have) to hurry to get things ready for my party now if I _____ (not fall) asleep after lunch.
5 If I _____ (accept) that invitation to her party, I _____ (be) at her flat in London now.
6 I _____ (not need) to work so hard now if I _____ (study) a lot more last term.
7 I _____ (feel) very guilty now if I _____ (forget) my mother's birthday, so I'm really happy that I remembered!
8 Jeremy hasn't phoned me, but if he _____ (not miss) the flight last night he _____ (be) here now.

4 ★★★ **Complete the sentences so they are true for you. Use mixed conditionals.**

1 If I wasn't studying English now I _____
_____
2 I wouldn't be _____
_____
3 If I had _____
_____
4 If I hadn't _____
_____
5 I would _____
_____
6 If I were _____
_____

Alternatives to *if* SB page 35

5 ★★ **Cross out the word or words which do NOT fit.**

0 We can go in my car ~~otherwise~~ / *as long as* / ~~unless~~ we share the cost of petrol.

1 I wouldn't interrupt Mum now *unless* / *if* / *otherwise* you want her to get really angry.

2 *Suppose* / *Imagine* / *As long as* you could visit another planet, where would you go?

3 Eat your soup now, *suppose* / *unless* / *otherwise* it'll get cold.

4 *Unless* / *If* / *Otherwise* you can't get to the front of the crowd, you won't see much of the parade.

5 Of course you can borrow my book, *as long as* / *unless* / *provided that* you don't lose it.

6 *Imagine* / *Provided that* / *Suppose* you get there early, there will be plenty of space to sit.

6 ★★ **Complete the dialogue with the words/phrases in the list. Use each one only once.**

unless | Imagine | provided that
as long as | otherwise | Suppose | if

MAY My brother won't eat vegetables
¹_____ they're green.

DAN Why?

MAY He says green is his lucky colour, so ²_____ Mum gives him green vegetables, he's OK.

DAN ³_____ she gave him carrots, what would he do?

MAY He'd refuse to eat them.

DAN ⁴_____ she could dye them green – what then?

MAY Yeah, that might work. But only if she told him they were special beans or something, ⁵_____ he wouldn't eat them.

DAN Well, ⁶_____ that's the only thing he's picky about eating, then that's a good thing! His lucky colour could be brown – he would only eat chocolate!

MAY Well, I suppose you're right, ⁷_____ he grows out of it soon. I'm sick of only eating green vegetables at home.

7 ★★ **Re-write the rules using the words in brackets.**

RULES FOR RESIDENTS

1 You can come in after 11 pm. But tell the porter when you leave.

2 You mustn't leave your bicycle on the lawn if you are not going out immediately.

3 You can have a wake–up call in the morning, just tell the night porter.

4 You can use the kitchen but please leave it clean and tidy.

5 Keep your key safe. If you don't, you might get locked out.

6 Please only use the college phone in an emergency.

1 (as long as) _____

2 (unless) _____

3 (if) _____

4 (provided that) _____

5 (otherwise) _____

6 (unless) _____

GET IT RIGHT!

unless

Learners often use *unless* with a negative verb form when they should use a positive form.

✓ *Unless you **do** your homework, you can't play your game.*

✗ *Unless you ~~don't do~~ your homework, you can't play your game.*

Tick the sentences which are correct and rewrite the incorrect ones.

1 Unless you don't play the lottery, you don't have a chance of winning it! ☐

_____

2 We can deliver it next week, unless you need it tomorrow. ☐

_____

3 Jack's going to miss the beginning of the film unless he doesn't turn up in the next two minutes. ☐

_____

4 I will take you up on your offer unless you've changed your mind. ☐

_____

5 Sarah never travels on a Friday unless she absolutely doesn't have to. ☐

_____

Pronunciation

Unstressed words in connected speech
Go to page 118.

VOCABULARY

Phrasal verbs

break down | pull up | stand out | step in | take on | take up | turn out | turn up

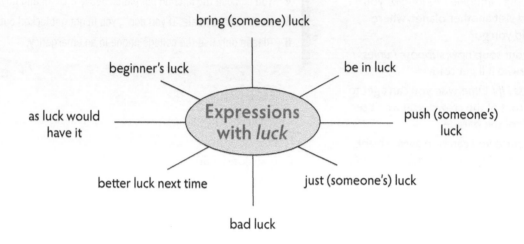

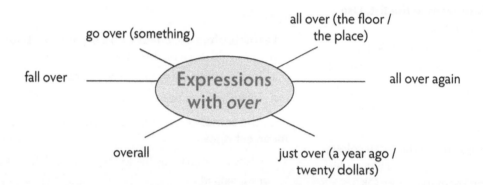

Key words in context

eradicate	In the past, polio was a fatal disease, but now it's been almost **eradicated**.
frantically	I couldn't find my keys anywhere, and I spent 20 minutes **frantically** looking for them.
horrendous	The weather was really bad – in fact, it was **horrendous**.
hurtle	A car **hurtled** towards us – I reckon it was doing over 120 km an hour.
numerous	I know the city quite well because I've been there on **numerous** occasions.
perspective	He's happy that he won, but from my **perspective**, it was a bad result.
recite	It's a poem I learned at school – I can **recite** it from beginning to end.
reckless	He was riding his bike the wrong way up a one-way street – he's so **reckless**!
rehearse	I know exactly what I'm going to say tomorrow – I've **rehearsed** it ten times!
sip	The coffee was very hot so to start I just **sipped** it very slowly.
soothing	This music helps me relax and go to sleep – it's very **soothing**.
swerve	A pedestrian walked out in front of my car and I had to **swerve** to avoid her.

Phrasal verbs SB page 32

1 ★★ Complete the crossword.

1 I couldn't play in the band that night, so my friend … in and played instead.

2 She needed something new in her life, so she … up the piano.

3 I was in the town centre when a car … up and the driver asked me for directions.

4 You don't have to buy tickets in advance, just … up and you'll get in.

5 I was late for work because the bus … down.

6 All the competitors were good, but she really … out.

7 I was sure he was German, but it … out I was wrong – he was Swiss.

8 No one else wanted to do the work, so I've … it on.

2 ★★ Complete the sentences with a phrasal verb in the correct form.

1 Our car is old and useless! It _____ at least once a week.

2 The weather forecast said it would rain, but the day _____ to be really nice!

3 I've got so much work to do – I don't think I can _____ any more.

4 The main actor got ill, so I _____ and played the part.

5 Mum? Can we _____ outside that shop so I can get some chocolate?

6 She's very tall, so she _____ when she's with her shorter friends.

7 Last year I became interested in birds, so I _____ birdwatching.

8 I thought only about ten people would come – but over fifty people _____!

Expressions with *luck* SB page 33

3 ★ Complete the phrases with one word.

1 Oh dear, _____ luck

2 You're _____ your luck

3 And I thought: It's _____ my luck

4 She was _____ luck

5 They didn't _____ me any luck

6 It's just _____ luck

7 As luck would _____ it

8 _____ luck next time

4 ★★ Match the responses in Exercise 3 to the statements/questions.

0 A I just missed the bus!
  B [*1*]!

1 A You've never played this before – and you won?
  B I know. Sorry! [ ].

2 A So your sister met the rock star?
  B Yes. They were staying at the same hotel. [ ].

3 A Did you try to buy a ticket for the concert?
  B Yes. But they had sold out. [ ].

4 A So your car broke down?
  B Yes. [ ], though, we were very close to a garage.

5 A Dad, can you lend me another £20?
  B Wow. [ ]

6 A Did you wear your lucky shorts for the game?
  B I did. [ ], though. I lost!

7 A I failed my driving test. Again!
  B I'm sorry to hear that. [ ].

WordWise SB page 37

Expressions with *over*

5 ★★ Complete the sentences with a phrase from the list.

all over | all over again | fall over
overall | just over | go over

1 My school's _____ a kilometre away so it's a quick bike ride for me.

2 Can we _____ it just once more?

3 Their new CD is so good that when I'd finished listening to it, I decided to listen to it _____.

4 The food was great, the service was OK, and it was very cheap – so, _____, it was a good dinner!

5 The water pipe to the washing machine leaked and there was water _____ the floor.

6 I was so tired, I thought I was going to _____ when I was going up the stairs to bed!

READING

1 **REMEMBER AND CHECK** Match the phrases from columns A, B and C. Then read the article on page 31 of the Student's Book again and check.

A	B	C
1 Amanda got her break into acting	but he arrived late because	that Janine was all right.
2 Amanda had learned	because another motorist	it got stuck in a traffic jam.
3 Jason's dad took a taxi	stopped to make sure	during the rehearsals.
4 Jason's dad was happy	when another actress	broke her leg.
5 Janine had to swerve off the road	that he missed the plane	because it crashed.
6 A man in another car	all the lines	was driving recklessly.

2 Read the story quickly. What was wrong with the car?

MY LUCKY DAY?

I guess just about everyone has a story like this one – about how luck, or fate, or something prevented you from suffering a terrible injury, or even dying. There must be thousands of people who missed the plane or train that crashed, or who walked out of a building moments before it blew up. Well, this is my story.

Many years ago, I was on the island of Sulawesi in Indonesia, working as a teacher on a country-wide project. I'd spent a few days in Palu, on the coast, working with the local manager, a lovely guy named Dudi. He said that the following day he planned to drive me about 250 kilometres into the interior of the island, to visit a school involved in the project. 'It's a long and difficult drive,' Dudi said, 'so if you don't want to go, just say.' But I told him I was more than happy to go and so he said he'd pick me up from my hotel early the next morning.

Dudi arrived promptly and we went to the car. We'd been driving around Palu in his small Honda, but that morning he turned up in a big Toyota 4x4. 'I've borrowed

it from a friend,' Dudi explained. 'It's better for the roads we'll be using. More comfortable, too. And yesterday we had it serviced, so everything's perfect.' Great! We got in and set off.

Leaving Palu, we drove along the coast for a while. It was a warm day, I had the window open, and I remember that two or three times, I thought I heard a kind of metallic 'click' and a pinging noise, but I didn't pay much attention to it. Soon after that, the road began to climb upwards – it was an extremely narrow, winding road, and when I looked out of the side window I could see that there was a valley below and nothing, absolutely nothing, between it and us. No fence, no barrier – nothing. Just a steep drop down into the valley below. 'Wow!' I thought. 'I really hope we keep on the road.'

Just then I heard a noise. I looked towards the front and there was a truck hurtling down the hill towards us, blasting his horn. Dudi looked aghast, hit the brakes and pulled the car over. We lurched to a halt and the truck went flying past.

We heard a thump. 'Let's check the car,' said Dudi, so we got out and started to look round. Then I heard Dudi say, 'Oh wow – come and look at this!' He'd gone pale. He was looking at the rear wheel – it had one single, lonely wheel nut on it, and the wheel was over at an angle. That noise I'd heard before? It was the five wheel nuts coming off one by one – the people at the garage who serviced the car hadn't tightened the nuts properly when they put the wheel back on. I looked down at the valley – if we hadn't stopped because of the truck, that last wheel nut would have come off, and the wheel would have come off too. We would have fallen down into the valley, and I don't think I'd be alive now. I've never felt so lucky in my life, before or after.

3 All these statements are incorrect. Correct them using the word in brackets.

1 The writer was working as a manager in Sulawesi. (teacher)

2 He didn't want to go on the drive. (happy)

3 They travelled in Dudi's new 4x4 Toyota. (belonged)

4 On the drive, the writer was worried by noises that he heard. (attention)

5 They stopped because a truck hit their car. (hurtling)

6 One wheel nut had come off each wheel. (five)

4 Choose one of the ideas below and write an 8–10 line dialogue.

A The writer and Dudi when they looked at the wheel

B Dudi and the people at the garage, three days later

DEVELOPING WRITING

A story about luck

1 Read the story and put the pictures in order.

2 Read again. Answer the questions.

1 In what two ways were the sunglasses important to the writer?

2 How did the writer feel when she discovered she hadn't got her sunglasses?

3 When did she realise she might find her glasses again?

4 How did the writer feel when she found the glasses?

3 Find words or phrases which:

1 are used to skip a part of the story.

2 show how the writer felt at several different moments.

4 You are going to write a short story about 'a bit of luck'. It can be something that happened to you or to someone you know, or a made-up story.

- What is the background to the story?
- What happened that was not good?
- What was the bit of luck that made things OK in the end?

5 Write your story in 250–300 words. Make sure to:

- think about the verb tenses you use;
- use at least one mixed conditional sentence;
- use adjectives / expressions showing how people felt at different moments in the story.

A bit of luck

One day I took a bus into town and even though it wasn't sunny, I was wearing my sunglasses. They're the best glasses ever. If I hadn't saved up for ages, I wouldn't have been able to buy them. To get to the point, I think I look really cool in them.

I sat down and took the glasses off to read my magazine. Well, to cut a long story short, when I got off the bus, I started to look for my glasses and … not there. My heart sank! I walked back towards the bus stop but they weren't on the ground. Somehow, I'd left them on the bus!

I don't think I've ever felt so miserable in my life. I looked in some shop windows, but all I wanted to do was go home. I started walking but then, just as I was near a bus stop, I saw a bus coming, so I got on it. As I was paying the driver, I realised he looked familiar. Was it possible? Was this the same bus I'd used to go into town? I ran to the back, and there, on the floor under a seat – my sunglasses! I was speechless, and over the moon. And I thought how lucky I was – if I hadn't seen the bus coming, I'd never have seen my glasses again.

CHECKLIST ✔

LISTENING

1　◀》10　Read the sentences below. Then listen and write the number of the conversation, 1, 2 or 3 in the boxes.

1　They are discussing how to replace something that was borrowed. ☐

2　They are discussing how to get somewhere without paying more than necessary. ☐

3　They are discussing the nature of quiz shows. ☐

2　◀》10　Listen again and complete the sentences with three words.

Conversation 1

1　Cheap train tickets to London _____ after nine o'clock.

2　Julie thinks arriving in London at 9.55 is _____ for her.

Conversation 2

3　Jamie likes the mixture of _____ in the quiz programme.

4　Sally prefers 'Mastermind' because contestants can _____ subject.

Conversation 3

5　Some of Paul's stuff got _____ when he dropped his bag.

6　Paul cannot replace the book because it costs _____ pounds.

DIALOGUE

1　Put the dialogue in the correct order.

☐ GINA　Yes, and it didn't come for ages. And when it finally did come, it got stuck in a traffic jam, you know, it being rush hour at that time of day and all.

☐ GINA　Not wrong exactly – just not right! I was hoping I'd be back home in time for my favourite show on TV, but the bus driver simply went past my stop without pulling over to pick me up! Just my luck.

1 GINA　Today hasn't been my lucky day.

☐ GINA　No, and my mum didn't think to record it either. And I so badly wanted to see it.

☐ MARTHA　So you had to wait for the next one?

☐ MARTHA　Oh? Why's that? Did something go wrong?

☐ MARTHA　Bad luck. But don't worry, I'm sure they'll show it again before too long and we can record it for you.

☐ MARTHA　It's always bad after five o'clock, isn't it? But anyway, I'm guessing you didn't make it back home in time for the show?

PHRASES FOR FLUENCY

SB page 37

1　Complete the phrases by adding the missing letters.

1　a___ m___g

2　t___ t i_

3　a___er a___

4　___ w a___d ___ain

5　W___ h___ you g___ to ___e?

6　We'll ___ t s___g o_t.

2　Complete the mini-dialogues with the phrases from Exercise 1.

1

A　I'm thinking about learning how to play chess. Do you think I'm mad?

B　Of course not. Go for it! _____

2

A　What time does your cousin arrive tomorrow?

B　He'll be here at 11 o'clock, _____ the train's on time.

3

A　Can I borrow your tablet?

B　Well, OK, provided you take really good care of it, _____.

4

A　You're listening to rap? I thought you were a rock fan!

B　Well, I am – but I don't mind a bit of rap _____, just for a change.

5

A　Hang on – how can we possibly go to the match and get back in time for the party tonight?

B　Yeah, it's tricky – but it's OK. _____.

6

A　You must be really pleased that you got 92%.

B　Yeah, kind of – but it was a really easy test, _____.

Listening Part 1

1 🔊 **11** You will hear three different extracts. For questions 1–6, choose the answer (A, B or C) which fits best according to what you hear. There are two questions for each extract.

Extract 1

You hear two friends discussing how they did in a Geography examination.

1 What aspect of the exam do the two friends disagree about?
  A How difficult the exam was
  B How fair the exam was
  C How useful the teacher's advice was before the exam

2 What does Maggie think about Daniel's results?
  A He should not complain about them.
  B He should keep his spirits up.
  C He has probably done better than he thinks.

Extract 2

You hear two people talking about a car accident involving the man's sister.

3 What was the principal cause of the accident?
  A A motorcyclist appeared unexpectedly.
  B Another car swerved and hit her at high speed.
  C The woman swerved because she was driving very fast.

4 What happened to the driver of the other car?
  A He was taken to hospital in an ambulance.
  B He was not hurt at all.
  C He was unconscious after the accident.

Extract 3

You hear two people talking about photographs of wild animals and birds.

5 What does the boy especially like about the photo of the eagle?
  A It's a photo of a very rare bird.
  B He took the photo at just the right moment.
  C He got so close to the bird.

6 What does he say about the relationship between equipment and skill?
  A The equipment is important but you need to have experience of using it.
  B You need both but luck is more important.
  C A 400 millimetre lens is what matters most.

GRAMMAR

Emphatic structures `SB page 40`

1 ★★☆ Complete the dialogue with *it's*, *what* or *all*. When there is a choice between *what* and *all*, think carefully which one is best.

DANA   I'm hungry. What shall we have for dinner?

SIMON   Not much. ¹_____ there is in the fridge are four eggs.

DANA   Well, ²_____ you need to make an omelette is an egg and a frying pan. Can you make one?

SIMON   Me? ³_____ always me who does the cooking.

DANA   That's because ⁴_____ me who goes to work all day.

SIMON   ⁵_____ I'd like to do is to go out for a meal.

DANA   Really? I'm quite tired. ⁶_____ I really want to do is stay in and watch TV.

SIMON   Again? Why don't we do something different for a change?

DANA   If you want me to cook, ⁷_____ you need to do is ask.

SIMON   No, ⁸_____ I want is to eat in a nice restaurant and then go and see a film at the cinema. We haven't been for months. ⁹_____ doing things like that together that I really miss.

DANA   OK, make me an omelette tonight and I promise we'll go out at the weekend.

2 ★★☆ Rewrite the sentences using emphatic structures and the words given.

What

0   He needs a good holiday.

   What he needs is a good holiday.

1   I like a joke with a good punchline.

   _____

It

2   Brian's good at telling jokes, not his brother.

   _____

3   You waste your time playing on your computer.

   _____

All

4   She was only saying that you should take a break.

   _____

5   Dave only wants a sandwich for lunch.

   _____

3 ★★★ Use cleft sentences to rewrite each pair of sentences using the underlined information as the focus. Use *it is / was* and *what* for each pair.

0   a   <u>David</u> ate your sandwich.

      It was David who ate your sandwich.

   b   David ate your <u>sandwich</u>.

      What David ate was your sandwich.

1   a   You need to say '<u>sorry</u>'.

      _____

   b   <u>You</u> need to say 'sorry'.

      _____

2   a   My <u>dad</u> forgot the punchline.

      _____

   b   My dad forgot the <u>punchline</u>.

      _____

3   a   <u>I don't understand</u> why she said 'no'.

      _____

   b   I don't understand <u>why she said 'no'</u>.

      _____

4   a   I hate <u>cold showers</u> more than anything.

      _____

   b   I <u>hate</u> cold showers <u>more than anything</u>.

      _____

Boosting SB page 43

4 ★ Match two sentences to each picture.

1 You've clearly never tried this before.
2 She's absolutely brilliant.
3 Well, it's undeniably the most unusual thing we've ever discovered.
4 She certainly knows how to entertain.
5 I've totally forgotten how to do this.
6 It's utterly delicious.
7 It's essentially half frog, half bird.
8 Well he definitely enjoyed that!

A

Cake Competition – judges

B

C

D

5 ★★ Rewrite the sentences to include the word in brackets.

1 This is the best day of my life. (undeniably)

2 I have made the best decision of my life. (certainly)

3 I am the happiest man on the planet. (undoubtedly)

4 It's what I've always wanted to do. (essentially)

5 I can't wait to get started. (definitely)

6 It is the job of my dreams. (literally)

7 A chocolate taster! I mean it's amazing. (utterly)

8 And this company makes the best chocolates there are. (absolutely)

6 ★★★ Use the prompts to write sentences that are true for you.

0 best day of my life / undeniably
The best day of my life was undeniably when I passed my driving test.

1 most interesting place in my town / undoubtedly

2 most interesting school subject / certainly

3 the best day of the week / clearly

4 my favourite holiday destination / absolutely

5 the best band in the world / unquestionably

6 my favourite actor / definitely

7 ★★★ Add reasons to your sentences in Exercise 6.

0 *It means that I can now go anywhere I like.*

GET IT RIGHT!
Emphatic sentences

Learners at this level often use a subject pronoun instead of an object pronoun in cleft sentences beginning with *It's* ... Another common error is using *it's ... what* instead of *it's ... that.*

✓ It's **her** who complains a lot. It's her attitude **that** really annoys me.

✗ It's ~~she~~ who complains a lot. It's her attitude ~~what~~ really annoys me.

Correct the errors in the sentences.

1 It's the release of endorphins what makes us feel good when we laugh.

2 It's his sense of humour what I don't get.

3 It's we who will have the last laugh when we win the tournament.

4 It's he that is undoubtedly the best comedian in the country at the moment.

5 It's they who will be laughing on the other side of their faces when their teacher finds out.

VOCABULARY

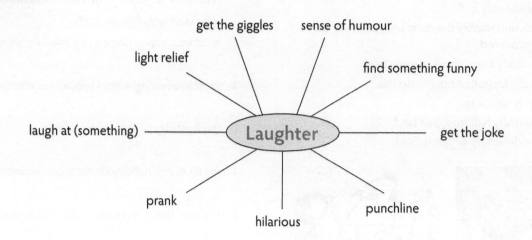

get the giggles   sense of humour

light relief

find something funny

laugh at (something) —— **Laughter** —— get the joke

prank

hilarious

punchline

Idioms with *laugh* and *joke*

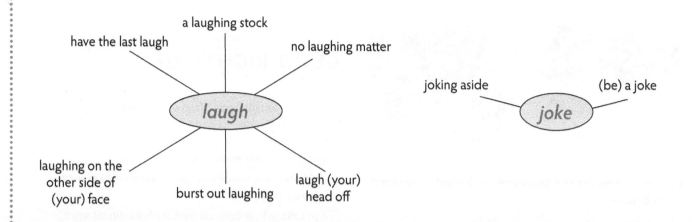

a laughing stock

have the last laugh

no laughing matter

laugh

laughing on the other side of (your) face

burst out laughing

laugh (your) head off

joking aside   **joke**   (be) a joke

Key words in context

assassinate	The attempt to **assassinate** the president failed when police arrested the gunman.
attributed	The poor exam results are being **attributed** to children not studying enough at home.
conditioned	Are children being **conditioned** by the games they play?
contagious	The disease is highly **contagious** and doctors warn against coming into contact with anyone who has it.
contradict	Mr Jones said the summer holiday starts on 7th June, but our headmaster **contradicted** him saying it was 8th June.
logic	Buying a car before you've learned how to drive – I don't see the **logic** in that.
make light of	It's a serious situation and you shouldn't **make light of** it.
outburst	No one understood the joke at first but then there was an **outburst** of laughter as people suddenly got it.
seemingly	No one knows where the money went. It just **seemingly** disappeared.
signalling	The referee blew his whistle, **signalling** an end to the match.
start out	He **started out** making tea for the directors. Now he owns the company.
unconsciously	I'm not sure why I did that. I did it totally **unconsciously**.

Laughter `SB page 40`

1 ★ **Match the sentence halves.**

1 Mr Thomas really has no sense of ☐

2 It was a silly prank and ☐

3 It's so embarrassing but sometimes I get ☐

4 I've told you not to laugh ☐

5 I'm sorry but I just don't find ☐

6 I like horror films that offer a little light ☐

7 He got right to the end of the joke
   and forgot ☐

8 That show was hilarious, ☐

9 I'm not really sure I got ☐

a it funny when you talk in that stupid voice.

b the punchline.

c I haven't laughed so much in a long time.

d relief at times to give you the chance to relax.

e you could have hurt someone.

f at Tim. You know it upsets him.

g the giggles in the middle of maths lessons.

h humour. In fact I've never even seen him
   smile.

i the joke but I laughed anyway.

2 ★★★ **Complete the questionnaire and then answer the questions.**

How good is your _____ of humour?

I What do you do if you don't _____ a joke?

_____

2 You are the victim of a mean _____.
  You're soaking wet. Everyone's laughing
  _____ you. How do you react?

_____

3 You're telling a joke. It's going well.
  Disaster – you've forgotten the
  _____! What do you do?

_____

4 It's the middle of an English lesson.
  You've got the _____. Your teacher
  wants to know what it is you _____
  so funny. What do you say?

Idioms with *laugh* and *joke* `SB page 43`

3 ★★ **Complete the mini-dialogues with *laugh(ed)*, *laughing*, *joke* or *joking*.**

1 A I'm thinking of entering your school's talent evening
     for parents.

   B Please don't, Dad. You'll be a _____ stock.

2 A Can you believe that Jack took his mum's car and he
     can't even drive?

   B It's no _____ matter, Liam. He got stopped by the
     police and now he's in big trouble.

3 A Did you watch that new comedy series I told you
     about?

   B I certainly did. I _____ my head off.

4 A Have you seen Dan's new haircut? Isn't it ridiculous?

   B I know. I just burst out _____ when I saw him.

5 A Don't worry, Mum. I'll just eat oven chips every day.

   B _____ aside, Will, do you really think you'll be
     able to look after yourself if you move out?

6 A £700 on a flight to Brazil and now the airline wants to
     charge me another £30 to choose my seat.

   B I know. It's a _____.

7 A That couple think it's funny to keep calling me over to
     their table.

   B Don't worry, they'll be _____ on the other side of
     their faces when they get their bill.

8 A My friends all think it's funny that I didn't get into
     university.

   B Don't worry. You'll have the last _____ when
     you're a millionaire at 25 while they're all paying off
     their student loans.

4 ★★★ **Complete the sentences with your own ideas.**

1 He might think it's funny to mess about in class but
  he'll be laughing on the other side of his face when
  _____.

2 I couldn't help myself. I just burst out laughing when
  _____.

3 I can't believe _____. It's a joke.

4 Don't _____.
  You'll be a laughing stock.

5 Why are you giggling? It's no laughing matter when
  _____.

6 I laugh my head off every time
  _____.

7 I know you think it's silly that I want to swim
  across the Channel for charity, but joking aside,
  _____.

8 So you didn't get a part in the school play? Well you'll
  have the last laugh when _____.

READING

1 REMEMBER AND CHECK Mark the sentences T (true) or F (false). Then read the article on page 39 of the Student's Book again and check.

1 Children tend to have a better sense of humour than adults. ☐

2 As we get older we tend to care less about what people think of us. ☐

3 Laughter is more effective in the company of others. ☐

4 Laughter is often provoked by unpredictable things. ☐

5 We might laugh at someone having an accident as we feel relieved it didn't happen to us. ☐

6 Laughter can help us cope with the more unpleasant things in life. ☐

2 Read the article. What are the main benefits of laughter therapy? _____

Laughter therapy

Laughter not only provides a full-scale workout for your muscles, it unleashes a rush of stress-busting endorphins. What's more, your body can't distinguish between real and fake laughter – any giggle will do.

A ☐ The elation, or extreme happiness, you feel when you laugh is a great way of fighting the physical effects of stress. When we laugh, our body relaxes and endorphins (natural painkillers) are released into the blood stream.

A Laughter Therapist's aim is to help you laugh more easily. Therapy is available in group or individual sessions – these start with a warm-up followed by a range of activities designed to get you giggling. Laughter doesn't come easily to everyone, but luckily the body can't actually tell the difference between real and fake laughter. So faking it has the same beneficial effect.

B ☐ Dr Lee Berk of Loma University Medical Centre, California, has been conducting laughter therapy research since the late 1970s. In 1989, Berk studied the effects of laughter in 10 healthy males. Five experimental subjects watched an hour-long comedy while five control subjects didn't. Blood samples taken from the 10 subjects revealed that cortisol (the hormone our body releases when under stress) in the experimental subjects had decreased more rapidly in comparison to the control group. Berk's research has also shown the number of cells that attack viruses and tumours increases through laughter. These same cells are blocked if the body suffers long-term stress.

Researchers at the University of Michigan have also calculated that just 20 seconds of laughter could be as good for the lungs as three minutes spent on a rowing machine.

C ☐ The therapeutic effects of laughter have been clinically studied since the 70s, but Dr Madan Kataria – who developed laughter yoga in Mumbai – is credited with making laughter therapy more well-known. Kataria set up the first laughter club in 1995. There are now more than 5,000 laughter clubs worldwide.

D ☐ Laughter therapy is suitable for everyone although most therapists work within the healthcare profession or in the workplace, where laughter is used as a means of relieving stress.

Elderly groups, young people in care and mental health patients are all thought to benefit especially from laughter therapy. If you're undecided, remember this: children laugh about 400 times a day whereas adults manage a mere 15.

E ☐ A laughter therapy session may leave you feeling elated and exhausted in equal measure. Muscle tone and cardiovascular functions may be improved, and oxygen levels in the blood may be boosted.

In the long term, laughter therapy teaches us that we don't just have to laugh when we are happy. Laughing in the face of anger, stress or anxiety – even if it's forced laughter – can actually lift your mood. And it's contagious, so you can expect to see those around you benefiting from a good giggle too.

3 Read the article again and match the headings with the paragraphs. There is one extra heading.

1 Is there any evidence?

2 What is it?

3 Is it just a fad?

4 What results can I expect?

5 Where does it come from?

6 Who can do it?

4 What do you think about laughter therapy? Write a short paragraph explaining whether you think it would be good for you. Give your reasons.

DEVELOPING WRITING

A review

1 **Read the review. Which of the following does it NOT mention?**

the characters	☐	the plot	☐
the actors	☐	the dialogue	☐
setting	☐	the soundtrack	☐

2 **Choose three of the boosting adverbs and decide where you could put them in the review. There are several possibilities.**

~~undeniably~~ | clearly | absolutely | definitely
entirely | undoubtedly | essentially | utterly
literally | totally | unquestionably | certainly

3 **Read the review again and answer the questions.**

Paragraph 1

1 What factual information does the reviewer include in his introduction?

_____

Paragraph 2

2 Why does the reviewer say 'In case...'?

_____

3 What is the purpose of this paragraph?

_____

Paragraph 3

4 What does the reviewer find unoriginal about the show?

_____

5 What does the reviewer like about the show?

_____

Paragraph 4

6 What relevance to our own lives does the writer feel the show has?

_____

4 **Write a review of a TV or Internet comedy series. Write 220–260 words.**

CHECKLIST ✓

Writing tip: reviews

- In your introduction, try to answer *Wh-* questions. This will give your reader a good idea of what your subject is about. You might not be able to answer them all so choose the most relevant for your review.

- Don't give any spoilers (information that might ruin it for someone who hasn't seen it yet) and especially don't give away the ending. You might want to introduce a teaser though. This information doesn't give anything away, but will make the reader interested to find out more.

- When you give your recommendations, be definitive – use extreme adjectives. Remember your job is to try to convince the reader one way or the other.

- Use cleft sentences to add greater emphasis.

undeniably
It takes a special kind of series to make it to a ninth season. *Seinfeld* managed it, *Friends* went one better and as *The Big Bang Theory* embarks on this milestone, no one would be surprised if it went on for a few more.

In case you have never seen an episode, *The Big Bang Theory* follows the fortunes of four extremely intelligent but socially awkward scientists; Sheldon and Leonard (who share an apartment) and their friends Howard and Rajesh. When not working, the four hang out together playing video games, buying comic books or watching sci-fi films. This cosy, nerdy male world is turned upside down when the beautiful Penny moves in across the hall from Leonard and Sheldon.

In terms of its basic 'boy meets girl' premise, *The Big Bang Theory* is nothing new. Neither is the 'opposites attract' idea original. But then the show isn't really trying to redefine the genre. What *The Big Bang Theory* delivers so well are clever storylines, sharply written lines of conversation and, above all, well-rounded and lovable characters. One character in particular has helped transform the show into such a global hit. With his deeply unconventional mannerisms and highly literal take on life, Sheldon has become a firm favourite with fans.

I must admit that it took me a while to get into *The Big Bang Theory*, probably because it involved a world that I have little experience of. But I'm happy I stuck with it because now I feel completely at home with this adorable cast of characters and the challenges they face. After all, these challenges aren't so different to the ones we all encounter in our daily lives.

LISTENING

1 🔊12 **Listen and write the answers to the jokes.**

1 *What gets wetter the more it dries?*

_____

2 *What animal can jump higher than the Eiffel Tower?*

_____

3 Teacher: *What is the chemical formula for water?*

Student: *HIJKLMNO.*

Teacher: *What are you talking about?*

Student: _____

4 *What did the man say when he walked into a bar?*

_____

2 🔊12 **Listen again and answer the questions.**

Conversation 1

1 Why doesn't Lidia find the joke funny?

_____

2 What does Carl decide at the end?

_____

Conversation 2

3 What do both dads agree is the best thing about having young children?

_____

4 Where does Nat get all his jokes from?

_____

Conversation 3

5 What does Susie want help with?

_____

6 Why is Susie surprised by her mum's joke?

_____

Conversation 4

7 What has Jim got a reputation for?

_____

8 What's the answer to the joke about the kidnapping at school?

_____

3 **Complete the lines from the conversations with the missing words.**

1 I heard what you said. I just _____.

2 Ha ha, _____. I'll have to tell that one to Nat. He'll love it.

3 That's _____. I'm going to tell that to Mr Owens tomorrow.

4 Ouch. Of course. I like that. I _____ that one.

DIALOGUE

1 **Put the dialogue in order to make the joke.**

☐	TEACHER	Ok, let me put it to you differently. If I gave you two apples, and another two apples and another two, how many would you have?
☐	TEACHER	No, listen carefully … If I gave you two cats, and another two cats and another two, how many would you have?
1	TEACHER	If I gave you 2 cats and another 2 cats and another 2, how many would you have?
☐	TEACHER	Johnny, where on earth do you get seven from?
☐	TEACHER	Good. Now if I gave you two cats, and another two cats and another two, how many would you have?
☐	TOMMY	I've already told you. I'd have seven.
☐	TOMMY	For the third time, I'd have seven.
☐	TOMMY	Because I've already got a cat!
☐	TOMMY	Six apples.
☐	TOMMY	Easy. I'd have seven cats.

2 **Write a short dialogue of 8 to 10 lines that includes a joke in it.**

_____

_____

_____

_____

_____

_____

_____

_____

Pronunciation

Telling jokes: pacing, pausing and punchlines
Go to page 118. 🔊

Listening Part 3

Exam guide: multiple-choice questions

In this part of the exam you will hear an interview or an exchange between two or more people.

- The rubric will give you some information about who and where these people are. This will help you prepare yourself for the kind of recording you will hear.
- On the exam paper there are six multiple choice questions each with four possible answers from which you must choose the correct answer.
- You will have time before you listen so use this wisely to carefully read though the questions. This will help prepare you for the content of the listening. It is also a good idea to underline the key points in the questions to help you focus better.
- You will need to listen out for attitude, opinion, agreement, gist, feeling, speaker purpose, function and detail.
- You will hear the recording twice so use your second listening to confirm answers you already have and choose the best answers for those you didn't manage to get on the first listening.

1 ◁)) 14 **You will hear an interview in which two comedians, Paula Owens and Dave Sharp, are talking about their work. For questions 1–6, choose the answer (A, B, C or D) which fits best according to what you hear.**

1 What inspired Paula to make her first appearance?
   A The idea of being able to work on stage with a good friend of hers.
   B Comments from her friends and family.
   C The opportunity to collaborate with someone she found funny.
   D The desire to prove that she could do something despite leaving school with bad exam results.

2 What does she say about her early audiences?
   A Some members could be quite hostile towards the comedian.
   B They were extremely loyal.
   C They found her extremely funny.
   D They were generally on your side if you were not mean to them.

3 How did the theatre manager help her in her career?
   A He put her in touch with someone who could give her practical advice.
   B He told her about a club where they had regular comedy evenings.
   C He made her believe that she was good enough to be on stage.
   D He told her she was born to be on stage.

4 What does Dave say about his early experiences in comedy?
   A He was pretty nervous the first time he went on stage.
   B He really enjoyed making the audiences laugh.
   C It was much more difficult than he had expected it to be.
   D He found it difficult to complete the shows.

5 Paula and Dave agree that a comedian needs …
   A someone to tell them how good their jokes are.
   B a huge amount of energy.
   C to not care too much about what people say.
   D someone to organise you.

6 When it comes to the future both Paula and Dave …
   A believe you need to be topical if you want to survive as a comic.
   B fancy working in films.
   C hope to make a living from comedy.
   D are performing at an important comedy festival soon.

CONSOLIDATION

LISTENING

1 🔊 15 **Listen and put the events in the order Rosie mentions them.**

Order of mention		Chronological order
☐	Rosie gets injured.	☐
☐	Rosie misses the school bus.	☐
☐	Rosie revises for her test.	☐
☐	Rosie's school bus breaks down.	☐
☐	Rosie's phone runs out of battery.	☐
☐	Rosie tries to have a hot bath.	☐
☐	Rosie finds out that the headmaster is teaching her class.	☐
☐	Rosie forgets her packed lunch.	☐
☐	Rosie is locked out of the house.	☐

2 🔊 15 **Listen again and put the events above in chronological order.**

GRAMMAR

3 **Rewrite the sentences using the first word provided below.**

1 John bought a new tablet. That's why he's got no money.
   If _____

2 If we don't leave now, we'll miss the train.
   Unless _____

3 The food was the only thing I liked about the party.
   All _____

4 I don't like seafood. That's why I didn't eat anything at the restaurant.
   If I _____

5 You have to invite Sara to your party. Otherwise she'll be really upset.
   If _____

6 I find waiting for hours in airports the most annoying thing about travelling.
   What _____

7 You really need to talk to Henry about the mess.
   It's _____

8 I'll tell you my secret as long as you promise not to tell anyone.
   Provided _____

VOCABULARY

4 **Complete with *laugh*, *joke* or *luck*.**

1 I win again. Better _____ next time.

2 They think you're crazy for training every day after school but you'll have the last _____ when you get onto the national team.

3 It was a really good _____ but I can't remember the punchline.

4 £10 is my final offer. It's a good price so don't push your _____ .

5 Maybe I didn't get it but I didn't think that _____ was very funny.

6 It's raining and my umbrella's at home. That's just my _____ .

7 Change for a £10 note? Let me see. You're in _____ . Here you are.

8 £5 for a can of cola. That's a _____ , right?

5 **Match the sentence halves.**

1 My new job's great but I have taken ☐

2 Careful you don't fall ☐

3 This is the fifth time we've been ☐

4 Julia was wearing a bright red dress and really stood ☐

5 I felt bad but I couldn't help but burst ☐

6 If you're bored all the time why don't you take ☐

7 It's not kind to laugh ☐

8 The event was a great success and about 500 people turned ☐

a up a new hobby to fill up your time?

b over the dog when you leave.

c up to welcome the new headmaster.

d at him when he's learning to drive.

e on a lot more responsibility.

f out laughing when Dad walked into the door.

g over this and you still don't understand.

h out among the other party guests.

DIALOGUE

6 Put the dialogue in order.

	ROBIN	Ha ha. Very funny.
	ROBIN	Of course it does, assuming you believe in these things, that is.
	ROBIN	Don't mention it. Let's call it £5.
	ROBIN	Well, if I didn't have this coin, I certainly wouldn't have passed the mid-term exams.
1	ROBIN	Have I shown you my lucky pound coin?
	ROBIN	No, I'm serious. It's a bargain. It really works. What have you got to lose?
	ROBIN	Well you can have this one, if you want.
	JENNY	Only £4.
	JENNY	I do. I really do. So how has it helped you?
	JENNY	£5! Ha! That's a good one, Robin.
	JENNY	Really? I could do with something like that.
	JENNY	No you haven't, does it work?
	JENNY	Wow. Thanks. That's really kind of you.

READING

7 Read the article and answer the questions.

1 Why was the Laugh Lab set up?

2 What were visitors to the Laugh Lab's site asked to do?

3 What differences did they find in the European sense of humour and the English speaking world's sense of humour?

4 What rather unusual facts did the survey discover?

WRITING

8 What is your favourite joke? Translate it into English and write it down. Does it still sound funny?

The Laugh Lab

was an ambitious online scientific investigation into the nature of humour in an attempt to find out what makes us laugh and why. Among other things, it set out to discover the world's funniest joke, whether there was a difference in what the sexes found funny, how age affects our sense of humour and how different nationalities respond to different types of joke.

For one year The Laugh Lab's online site was visited by thousands of people from all over the world. They were asked to submit their favourite joke before going on to answer questions about themselves such as their age, sex and nationality. They were also asked to rate a number of jokes sent in by others using a specially designed 'giggleometer'. From a database of over 40,000 jokes and 1.5 million ratings, the researchers were able to draw some pretty definitive conclusions. For example …

The Germans were found to have the best sense of humour and laughed readily at a variety of different types of joke. They were followed by the French and the Danish. English-speaking countries such as the UK, the US, New Zealand and Australia tended to enjoy jokes which involved word-play such as:

Patient: Doctor, doctor. I keep thinking I'm a bridge.
Doctor: What's come over you?
Patient: Two cars, a lorry and a motorbike.

Many Europeans, on the other hand, tended to go for more surrealist jokes such as:

A dog went to a telegram office, took out a blank form and wrote:
'Woof. Woof. Woof. Woof. Woof. Woof. Woof. Woof. Woof.'
The clerk examined the paper and politely told the dog: 'There are only nine words here. You could send another 'Woof' for the same price.''But,' the dog replied, 'that would make no sense at all.'

The survey also came up with a number of more bizarre findings.

For example, it discovered that the time of day and the day of the month also had an effect on how funny a joke was found to be. It determined that the ideal time to tell a joke was 6.03 pm on the 15th of any month. It also found that the perfect length for a joke was 103 words and that the funniest animal in jokes was the duck.

5 | THRILL SEEKERS

GRAMMAR
Participle clauses SB page 50

1 ★☆☆ **Read the email about a day out in the Cheddar Gorge in England. Some of the participles in italics need to be changed to a past participle. Circle the 5 mistakes.**

> ¹*Feeling* adventurous, my friend and I booked a day of climbing and caving at Cheddar Gorge. ²*Not being* an experienced climber, I felt a bit nervous about the day. ³*Not liking being* in small spaces, my friend was also nervous. ⁴*Advising* by a friend, we chose to go with a company called Rocksport. That morning, ⁵*dressing* in overalls, boots and hats we headed for the caves with our instructor. ⁶*Seeing* the ladders descending down into the darkness, the adrenalin kicked in. ⁷*Crawling* through small gaps in the rock was sometimes scary, but overall I enjoyed the experience. After lunch we went climbing. ⁸*Encouraging* by the instructor, we cautiously ascended the rock face. ⁹*Warning* by a friend, I didn't look down – not even once. On finally ¹⁰*reaching* the top, I felt an overwhelming sense of achievement. Then ¹¹*abseiling* back down was great fun. ¹²*Filming* by a friend on the ground, I have a lovely record of that memorable afternoon.

2 ★★☆ **Choose the past or present participle to complete the sentences.**

1 *Motivating / Motivated* by the video, I decided to try zip-wiring.
2 *Paragliding / Paraglided* towards the beach, I felt the biggest thrill of my life.
3 *Going / Gone* into the cave, I felt my heart beat faster and faster.
4 *Inspiring / Inspired* by my father, I decided to climb Mount Everest.
5 *Training / Trained* by an expert, he was ready to do the jump.
6 *Watching / Watched* my brother abseil down the side of the building, I started to get really nervous.
7 *Climbing / Climbed* back down the cliff, I had to concentrate on not looking down.
8 *Surrounding / Surrounded* by mountains, this was the perfect place for a climbing school.

3 ★★☆ **Complete the text with the correct form of the verbs in brackets.**

While ¹_____ (climb) a cliff face in Cornwall, Max Kidman's safety rope broke. ²_____ (fall) 30 metres, he luckily landed on some grass which saved his life. However, ³_____ (break) his leg, he was unable to climb down to the beach. ⁴_____ (watch) by his family and friends, he was rescued by helicopter. Then, ⁵_____ (take) to hospital by the helicopter, he felt lucky to be alive. ⁶_____ (phone) the emergency services had saved his life. Later, when ⁷_____ (interview) by a reporter from a local newspaper, he gave an account of the events. '⁸_____ (have) this accident won't stop me from climbing again,' he said.

4 ★★☆ **Rewrite the sentences using a perfect participle.**

0 'I've paraglided before. I'm not scared,' she said.
   Having paraglided before, she wasn't scared.

1 'I've watched the video lots of times, so I know what happens,' he said.
   _____

2 'I've been scuba diving and now I'd like to try deep sea diving,' she said.
   _____

3 'I enjoyed caving in Wales, I want to do it again,' he said.
   _____

4 'I've worked as a stuntman in films, so I'm used to performing dangerous stunts,' he said.
   _____

5 'I've never been keen on heights so I don't think I can do a bungee jump,' she said.
   _____

5 ★★ Rewrite the sentences by turning the underlined part of the sentence into a participle clause.

1 <u>I trained for six months.</u> I was ready to run the marathon.

_____

2 <u>I watched the video.</u> It reminded me of the parachute jump.

_____

3 <u>He climbed Mount Kilimanjaro.</u> He was ready to climb Mount Everest.

_____

4 <u>She was afraid of heights.</u> She couldn't look down.

_____

5 <u>He was trained by an Olympic athlete.</u> He was strong and fit enough to trek across the desert.

_____

6 <u>She had done a bungee jump before.</u> She wasn't worried.

_____

6 ★★ Use the prompts to write sentences with a present participle and *while*, *after*, *since* or *on*. More than one answer is possible.

0 ski / on holiday / I / break / my leg
   While skiing on holiday, I broke my leg.

1 practise / on / an indoor climbing wall / I / ready / to climb / outdoors

_____

2 sign up for / a parachute jump / he / not able to sleep

_____

3 learn / her daughter / win / the marathon / she / be / very proud

_____

4 break / his leg / he / not do / any more climbing

_____

5 do / her first parachute jump / she / do / three more jumps / for charity

_____

6 watch / a film / set in the Alps / she / decide / join / a climbing club

_____

7 see / his friend / be afraid / he / climb back up / to help / him

_____

Verbs of perception with infinitive or gerund SB page 53

7 ★★ Complete the sentences with the infinitive or gerund of the verbs in the list.

blow | grip | beat | shine | fall | laugh

1 He felt a cold wind _____ across his face. Then he started to run.

2 We could hear people _____ so we knew they were enjoying the show.

3 If you look out of the window now, you can still see the sun _____ on the walls of the castle.

4 I was scared. I could feel my heart _____ very fast.

5 We could hear raindrops _____ on the rooftop.

6 I felt his hand _____ my arm as he tried to stop me. I pulled my arm away and I carried on running.

GET IT RIGHT!
Participle clauses

Learners often make mistakes with participle clauses. When wanting to indicate that an activity happened after another, *having* + past participle is necessary whereas if the activities happened at the same time a present participle is required.

✓ **Having finished** his project, James then went home.

✗ ~~Finishing~~ his project, James then went home.

Rewrite the sentences using a participle clause. Change the verb in bold to become the participle.

0 The stuntwoman **leapt** from the top of the building. Then she landed on some mattresses below.

   Having leapt from the top of the building, the
   stuntwoman landed on some mattresses below.

1 The risks **were minimised** so the film director decided to go ahead with the stunt.

_____

2 The teacher **made** his point loud and clear and told them they wouldn't pass the exam unless they revised.

_____

3 They **painted** Megan's bedroom and then bought new furniture for it.

_____

4 She **agreed** with us initially, but then told us that she wouldn't do it.

_____

5 Dan's mother **heard** him sing and felt very proud.

_____

6 Sam **did** one bungee jump and now can't wait to do another!

_____

VOCABULARY

Thrill seeking

nouns	adjectives	verbs
stunt	audacious	assess the risk
daredevil	death-defying	minimise the risk
risk-taker		get a kick out of

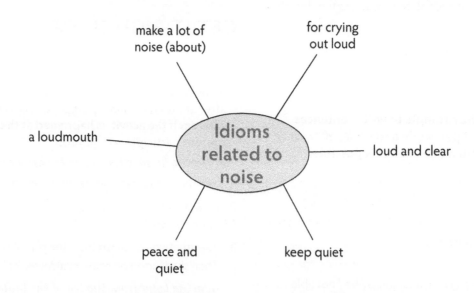

Key words in context

cautious	Sarah is very **cautious**. She doesn't like taking risks so I don't think she will want to come white-water rafting with us.
daring	I've become more **daring** as I've got older. Last year, I paraglided from a 1,969 metre mountain in Turkey.
enthusiast	My brother is a real speed **enthusiast**. He likes driving motorbikes and sports cars at high speed.
fatal	The blow to her head when she hit the rocks was **fatal**. She died in hospital later that day.
inspiration	My grandfather has always been an **inspiration** to me. He has done so many exciting things in his life.
multitude of	There are a **multitude of** different sports you can try.
overwhelmed	I was **overwhelmed** by my friends' support for my sponsored swim across Lake Windermere.
reassure	After the instructor had **reassured** me that it was completely safe, I began the climb.
stuntman	The **stuntman** performed a series of very dangerous jumps on a motorbike.
thrilling	On Saturday, I did a parachute jump. It was a **thrilling** experience. I'd love to do it again.

Thrill seeking SB page 51

1 ★ Match the words/phrases.

1	death-	a	the risk
2	dare	b	out of
3	minimise	c	devil
4	get a kick	d	taker
5	risk-	e	defying

2 ★★ Circle the correct words to complete the sentences.

1 That was an amazing *stunt / daredevil*! I didn't think he could cycle along that wall.

2 Susan isn't a *risk-taker / stunt*. She doesn't do anything unless she knows it's safe.

3 He performed one more *risk-taker / death-defying* stunt on his motorbike.

4 Sarah *gets a kick out of / assesses the risk of* base jumping. She really loves it.

5 The safety harness *assesses the risk / minimises the risk* of having an accident.

6 He is successful because he is *minimising the risks / audacious* and not afraid to take risks.

7 The instructor *assessed the risk / got a kick out of it* before we began the climb.

8 Matt's a complete *audacious / daredevil*. He's not scared of anything.

3 ★★ Complete the dialogue with the words/phrases in the list.

stunt | audacious | daredevil | death-defying
get a kick out of | assess the risk

ANNA Will you come and do a bungee jump with me?

MATT You're kidding. I can't think of anything worse.

ANNA Oh go on. You ¹_____ rollercoasters. And what about that amazing ²_____ on the skateboard you did on Saturday? That was a real ³_____ move.

MATT Yeah but a bungee jump's different. I'm not afraid of heights but I don't think I could do a bungee jump or go base jumping.

ANNA Come on, Matt. You're a ⁴_____. You love taking risks. You're an ⁵_____ climber.

MATT Yes, I take risks. But I always ⁶_____ before I do a skateboard stunt or climb a cliff face.

4 ★★★ Choose two of these questions to write about.

1 Describe the best stunt you've seen in a film.

2 What do you get a kick out of? Why?

3 Think of a dangerous activity. What are the risks involved and how can you minimise them?

4 Which of your friends is the biggest daredevil? What sort of things do they do?

Idioms related to noise SB page 53

5 ★★ Complete the mini-dialogues with 'noise' idioms.

1 A Have you seen this advert for the new hotel complex in our town?

 B Yes, they've been _____ about it in the local newspaper.

2 A Will you please turn off that music? I came in here for a bit of _____.

 B Sorry, Dad.

3 A Have you told Jake and Louise about your parachute jump?

 B No, and could you _____ about it for now? I'm still not sure I'm going to do the jump.

4 A Please don't tell Steve about this. You know what _____ he is. If you tell him, everyone will know about it.

 B I'm sorry, but I've already told him.

5 A The instructor's message was _____. Why didn't you listen to him?

 B I know, I know. But now I'm in this mess.

6 A _____, switch that TV off. You've been sitting in front of it all day.

 B OK, I will, after this programme finishes.

6 ★★★ Choose three of the expressions and write your own mini-dialogues.

1 A _____
 B _____

2 A _____
 B _____

3 A _____
 B _____

READING

1 **REMEMBER AND CHECK** Answer the questions. Then read the articles on page 49 of the Student's Book again and check.

1 What is Mrs Hardison the oldest female to have done?

2 How did Mrs Hardison celebrate her 90th birthday?

3 What has she motivated other members of her family to do?

4 What was Gary Connery the first man to do without a parachute?

5 Which structures has Gary Connery jumped from without a parachute?

6 Who did he dress up as at the 2012 Olympic opening ceremony?

2 Look at the photos. What one thing do you need to try any of these activities?

A a love of fear   B a love of heights   C immense skill   D climbing technique

---

⊝ ▢ ⊗   ◂ ▸ ⌂

FEEL THE FEAR

On April 21st 2009, the extreme kayaker, Tyler Bradt, kayaked over Washington's 57 metre-high Palouse Falls. He plunged over the waterfall in his canoe and survived the death-defying free-fall with just a broken paddle and a sprained wrist.

We can't all be Tyler Bradt but we can all be risk-takers in our own way. Here are just a few thrill-seeking adventures for all you daredevils out there to read about and imagine the adrenalin rush. Read on and feel the fear.

THE PLANK WALK – CHINA

On the 2,160 metre-high Mount Hua Shan in China, it has been called the deadliest hike in the world. It doesn't require any climbing skills, it just requires you to be a thrill-seeker with a love of fear.

You can either take a cable car to the mountaintop from Huayin or you can climb a steep stair route up the mountain that takes six hours. After that, there is another long hike before you get to the Plank walk itself. At this point you are 1,524 metres above the ground. Once you get to the Plank walk, however, you have to wear a harness, so yes, it's safe. It takes about 30 minutes to walk each way (there and back) along a narrow wooden plank on a terrifyingly steep cliff face with a sheer drop below.

As people are walking both ways on this path, you sometimes have to climb outside them and that can be scary. This sky walk is definitely not for the faint-hearted.

THE EDGE WALK – CANADA

You can test your fear of heights to the limit on the roof of Toronto's CN Tower's restaurant. With breath-taking views over Lake Ontario, the Edge Walk is a once in a lifetime experience. Where else can you lean back over Toronto with nothing but sky between you and the ground? The CN Tower is 356 metres tall and it has 116 storeys. Your sky stunt starts with a ride up to the roof restaurant in the lift. Then with six other people you attach yourself to an overhead safety rail to do the outdoor walk on the edge. The walk is about thirty minutes long and it's guaranteed to make your heart beat very fast.

THE FUJI-Q HIGHLAND AMUSEMENT PARK – JAPAN

The Fuji-Q Highland Amusement Park in Yamanashi, Japan is one of the most popular amusement parks for thrill-seekers and daredevils. Try Fujiyama, the longest and tallest rollercoaster in the park. It has a maximum speed of 130 km per hour, with a drop of 70 m, and a maximum height of 79 m. If that's not thrilling enough, you could try Dopdonpa which has a maximum speed of 170 km per hour and it has an almost vertical drop. Still not scary enough? There is the Eejanaik with its 14 inverted spins. If you get a kick out of going on rollercoasters, then the Fuji-Q Highland Amusement Park is the place for you.

---

3 Read the brochure and complete the sentences with between one and three words.

1 Tyler Bradt _____ Washington's Palouse Falls and survived.

2 The Plank walk is known as _____ in the world.

3 There is a drop of _____ below the plank.

4 The risks of falling are minimised on the Plank walk by ensuring that everyone has _____.

5 To reach the roof of the CN Tower in Toronto, you must _____.

6 The Fuji-Q Highland Amusement Park is great if you enjoy _____.

4 Write a short paragraph about a time you faced your fears.

How did you feel before, during and after the event? Describe your feelings.

Pronunciation

Connected speech feature: elision

Go to page 119. 🔊

DEVELOPING WRITING

An article

1 Read Sam's article for the school magazine about a tandem parachute jump for charity. Circle the correct participles.

2 Complete the article with the missing sentences.

   1 I heard cheering and clapping.
   2 I felt my legs shaking and my heart beating very fast.
   3 I could feel the wind whistling in my ears.

3 Read the article again and answer the questions.

   1 Why did Sam do the parachute jump?

   2 When did she do it?

   3 What two things did she need to put on?

   4 What made her feel more confident about jumping?

   5 When did she feel very nervous?

   6 Who was waiting for her on the ground?

   7 How did she describe the day?

4 Write an article in 200–250 words for your own school magazine about a thrilling experience.

Writing tip: an article

- Remember to answer all the *wh-* questions before you start your article.
- Use participle clauses to allow you to describe situations in a more concise way.
- Use verbs of perception to make your article more interesting.

CHECKLIST ✓

A Thrill to Remember

[1]*Motivated / Motivating* by my love of science, I volunteered to do a parachute jump to raise money for the new school science lab. It was a tandem parachute jump so I wouldn't be jumping alone.

After [2]*arriving / arrived* at the airfield on a warm sunny day in June, we were introduced to our instructors. Then, [3]*being given / having been given* a quick and easy introduction to skydiving, we got into our special jumpsuits. Then after [4]*fitting / fitted* the tandem parachute harness, we were ready to board the plane for the 15 minute ascent. [5]*Having known / Knowing* that I was securely attached to an experienced tandem instructor made me feel more confident. [6]*Feeling / Felt* only slightly nervous, I boarded the plane with my classmates and our instructors. However, as I waited my turn to jump out of the plane, **A** ☐ I was scared.

Finally, the moment came. I closed my eyes and we jumped. We were falling very fast – down and down we fell, and **B** ☐ Then at 1,066 metres the canopy opened. [7]*Having relaxing / Having relaxed* now, I started to enjoy the feeling of sailing high above the fields and houses. As we got closer to the ground **C** ☐ After [8]*landing / landed* with a thud on the soft grass, I felt a huge sense of relief. My friends, [9]*watched / watching* from the ground, ran to congratulate me.

[10]*Experienced / Having experienced* the thrill of skydiving once, I can't wait to do it again. We raised £1000 that day and I had one of the greatest experiences of my life.

LISTENING

1 🔊 **17** **Listen to the conversation. What do the numbers refer to?**

a 63   b 45   c 100

2 🔊 **17** **Listen again and answer the questions.**

1 What extraordinary thing have Will Gadd and Sarah Hueniken done?

_____

2 What have 15 other people done?

_____

3 What is Jane's opinion of Will and Sarah?

_____

4 What does Tony think about people who would do something like the climb?

_____

5 How long did the climb take Will and Sarah?

_____

6 What does Tony think is the best thing about the climb?

_____

3 🔊 **17** **Listen again and complete these parts of the conversation.**

1

JANE   She survived but she did say that no one should do that ever again.

TONY   _____. You'd be mad to throw yourself over a waterfall in a barrel.

JANE   _____, you've got to live a bit dangerously.

2

JANE   They've climbed a 45 metre-high frozen waterfall.

TONY   _____. That's a pretty cool achievement.

JANE   To come up with an idea like that. Then to plan it and organise it. Then to actually do it. That's awesome.

TONY   _____. However, I still think you have to be a little crazy to do something like that.

JANE   _____. I think they're incredibly brave.

3

JANE   I'm surprised they got permission from the authorities in the first place!

TONY   _____. How long did it take to get permission?

JANE   It took them a year.

TONY   _____, the best thing about it is getting to see these beautiful photographs of the ice falls.

JANE   _____. It's great that we get to share the view with Will and Sarah.

DIALOGUE

1 **Order the words to complete the dialogues.**

1

MARIA   Hi, Susie. How did your audition go yesterday?
it / hear / about / all / wait / can't / to / I

_____.

SUSIE   I don't think I'll get a part in the school play.

MARIA   come / actress / brilliant / You're / a / How / ?

_____.

SUSIE   I couldn't remember my lines. It was awful.

2

JAKE   Are you going to help me with the washing up, Sarah?

SARAH   No. I'm busy.

JAKE   But you never do anything around the house.

SARAH   no / here / go / we / Oh / ,

_____.

JAKE   You're always on your phone or on your laptop.
potato / into / a / couch / You're / turning

_____.

3

TONY   Why are you so tired, Joe?

JOE   I'm not sure.
go / did / I / sleep / to / late / really / last / night

_____.

I started browsing the Internet and I couldn't stop.

TONY   That explains it then.

JOE   What?

TONY   mean / I / know / You / what

_____.

You need to get some sleep. You should leave your phone in the living room at night. Problem solved.

2 **Write a dialogue of 8 to 10 lines. Disagree with a friend. Then accept his/her point.**

Your friend says that it's your fault that the team lost the football/tennis match on Saturday. You disagree.
OR
Your friend says you got too many answers wrong in the quiz so your team lost. You disagree.

Reading and Use of English Part 5

1 You are going to read a newspaper article about the first skydive over Mount Everest. For questions 1–6 choose the answer (A, B, C or D) which you think fits best according to the text.

1 The writer says that …

   A a woman filmed the skydive over Mount Everest.

   B only three people parachuted over Mount Everest.

   C one of the first three skydivers to parachute over Mount Everest was British.

   D the plane made a safe landing at 3,900 metres.

2 In Ms Budge's opinion, …

   A the fee was reasonable for such a once-in-a-lifetime experience.

   B the jump was vastly overpriced for what it was.

   C she would've paid more for the experience.

   D no one in their right minds would consider paying thousands of pounds to skydive off Everest.

3 The writer says that Alan Walton …

   A will not be allowed to jump as he is too old.

   B is on the list to jump in the next few days.

   C will probably be ready to skydive in a year's time.

   D wants to have his name added to the list of skydivers waiting to jump.

4 Mr Gifford, the organiser of the event, …

   A was not optimistic about the skydive.

   B decided that all participants should be experienced in both climbing and skydiving.

   C has tried both climbing and skydiving but has failed to bring them together.

   D has enjoyed bringing the two sports together.

5 How does Ms Smith describe her experience in the final paragraph?

   A The plain view of the mountains had made the whole experience seem truly unremarkable.

   B The scenery was magnificent and it was an astonishing feeling to be on top of the world.

   C The view of so many mountains was disappointing.

   D She had seen a view like this before.

6 Looking at the text as a whole, what best describes the overall experience of the skydive?

   A It was a complete success and everybody had a truly memorable and awe-inspiring experience.

   B On the whole people had a positive experience, but some people complained of the extreme cold.

   C Conditions were a lot worse than expected and people's high expectations were not met.

   D The expense of the trip ruined the experience.

BRITISH SKYDIVER MAKES FIRST JUMP OVER MOUNT EVEREST

A British skydiver has entered the record books as one of the first to parachute jump over Mount Everest towards the world's highest landing zone.

Adventurer Holly Budge, 29, described the experience as 'amazing, just spectacular' after making a safe landing at 3,900 metres. The Hampshire camerawoman was one of three skydivers in Nepal to make the first plunge from above the world's highest peak. 'We had one minute of freefall and while we were above the clouds you could see Everest and the other high mountains popping out of the top,' she said.

The trio, described by onlookers as looking 'like tiny birds flying in the blue sky', faced sub-zero temperatures and fast-changing weather when they touched down in the foothills of the mountain.

The event, organised by British adventure travel company High and Wild, will see up to 30 more skydivers from around the world perform the same feat in the coming days. Each of its clients has paid about £13,500 for the experience. 'It was worth the money – it is something that has never been done before,' said Ms Budge, who has completed 2,500 skydives and who jumped to raise money for charities in Britain and Nepal.

Skydiving at altitudes just higher than the summit of Mount Everest created numerous challenges for the project. Due to the thin air, their parachutes were three times the size of regular ones, and the jumpers used oxygen tanks strapped to their waists. They also wore undersuits and thermal gear to keep out the freezing temperatures as they leapt out at about 8,940 metres. 'The organisers have brought a plane over from Switzerland, and the permits have been very expensive, as has getting everyone to the jump site,' said Budge.

The oldest client due to make the jump in the coming days is Alan Walton, a 72-year-old British partner in a bioscience company, organiser Nigel Gifford said. 'Although many are very experienced, others are making their first ever skydive and will be going in tandem with experts,' said Gifford, whose company has permission to operate in the area for another 13 days.

The 'Everest Skydive' is an event that has been 15 years in the making for Mr Gifford. 'It came about because I have been a Himalayan mountaineer and took up skydiving. I love doing both and I thought it would be good to marry the two,' he said.

[...] Along with Ms Budge, the New Zealander Wendy Smith and Canadian Neil Jones were in freefall for nearly half a minute and then opened their canopies before landing on a flat drop zone after cruising over Everest.

New Zealand's Sir Edmund Hillary and Tenzing Norgay Sherpa first climbed Mount Everest's 8,850-metre peak 55 years ago. More than 3,000 climbers, among them a 16-year-old boy, a 76-year-old man, a man with an artificial limb and a blind person, have since reached the top of the mountain.

'It was stunning. I had never seen so many mountains before,' said Ms Smith. 'To be on top of the world was simply stunning. Thank you.'

6 FOLLOWERS

GRAMMAR

Modals 1: *may, might, can, could, will, won't* SB page 58

1 ★☆☆ **Decide if the underlined part of each sentence refers to the past (P), general time (GT) or the future (F).**

1 We <u>might</u> be right to say 'no' to nuclear weapons but I hope we won't be proved wrong. ☐

2 The cold weather <u>may</u> be the result of strong sea currents from the south. ☐

3 We <u>won't</u> know his answer until next week. ☐

4 I <u>will</u> give you a call when I arrive. ☐

5 Don't tell her too much. She <u>could</u> be a spy. ☐

6 I <u>could</u> see she was upset and I wanted to know if I could help. ☐

7 Dad <u>won't</u> give me any money so I can't go to the concert. ☐

8 Bears are very protective of their young and they <u>will</u> do anything to keep them safe. ☐

9 Following the England football team <u>can</u> be quite hard at times. ☐

10 Many fans <u>must</u> have been disappointed when she cancelled her show.

2 ★★☆ **Cross out the option in each sentence that is NOT possible.**

1 You *might / could / will* be forgiven for thinking he doesn't care but he's just really busy.

2 The strange lights that have been seen in the sky *might / may / can* just be aircraft.

3 The influence of Picasso on his work *might / can / could* be seen in his later paintings.

4 The fact he's not answering his phone *may / won't / could* mean he's lost it.

5 Dogs *will / can / could* act more aggressively when they are together.

6 My dad just *won't / doesn't / might not* listen to anything I say.

7 Their latest CD *can / may / might* just be their best.

8 We *couldn't / mightn't / didn't* understand a word that he said.

3 ★★☆ **Complete each pair of sentences with the same modal verb: *might, can, could, will* or *won't*.**

1 a Paul _____ return my phone calls. Have I done something to upset him?

 b I _____ be home before 8 o'clock so don't wait for me to eat.

2 a Changing school _____ be a very stressful time for any child.

 b Have you seen him play? He _____ do incredible things with a guitar.

3 a It _____ be many years before scientists finally find a cure for the disease.

 b I _____ name every capital city in the world when I was eight but I've forgotten most of them.

4 a Miss Dawes _____ always help you if she can.

 b I believe that it _____ soon be normal to live to 150.

5 a You _____ think she's a bit rude but the truth is she's very shy.

 b Owen _____ know the answer, he's pretty good at these things.

4 ★★★ **Complete the sentences with your own ideas.**

1 It's no good. He just won't _____

2 It's not a bad job but it can _____

3 Be careful. It might _____

4 I'm not sure this film will _____

Modals 2: *should, shouldn't, must, mustn't, can't* SB page 61

5 ★ Match the sentences.

1 He must know a lot of people. ☐
2 You must study harder. ☐
3 She shouldn't listen to such loud music. ☐
4 You shouldn't worry about me. ☐
5 You can't go in there. ☐
6 He can't be fifty. ☐
7 You mustn't eat the tomatoes. ☐
8 You mustn't get so nervous. ☐
9 You should give him a call. ☐
10 You should get on the train. ☐

a I'll be fine.
b He looks too young.
c I need them for dinner tonight.
d It'll spoil your performance.
e He'll be worried about you.
f I've never been to such a busy party.
g It's ready to leave.
h You're going to do badly in the exams if you don't.
i It's private property.
j She'll have problems with her hearing.

6 ★★ Read each pair of sentences. Match each sentence with its function. Mark the sentences E (expectations), S (strong advice), R (reasonableness) or A (advice).

0 She must be happy that she got the job. ☐ E
1 You must wear a hat today. ☐
2 It should be a nice day tomorrow. ☐
3 He can't be a professional singer. ☐
4 You should get a good night's sleep. ☐
5 We should have enough food for the picnic. ☐
6 You mustn't say a word. ☐
7 They mustn't get too worried. ☐
8 He shouldn't eat so much. ☐
9 You shouldn't expect him to answer your email immediately. ☐

7 ★★★ Write a follow on for each of the sentences in Exercise 6.

0 *She's always wanted to work in fashion.*
1
2
3
4
5
6
7
8
9

GET IT RIGHT! ⊙

Modals

Learners often confuse the different modals: *should, shouldn't, must, mustn't, can't, won't, would*.

✓ I don't think you **should** do that – it's wrong.
✗ I don't think you ~~must~~ do that – it's wrong.
✓ Ben **won't** come unless you ask him.
✗ Ben ~~mustn't~~ come unless you ask him.

Rewrite the sentences with the correct modal verb.

1 Do you think you would do that for me? I'd be very grateful.

2 That actress mustn't be invited on the chat show, surely? She's a has-been!

3 He should definitely try and keep a low profile if it meant he could keep the paparazzi away.

4 I can't imagine that any celebrity should ever wish to disappear without a trace.

5 Perhaps Julie would see a doctor about her total fixation on the royal family. It's not healthy.

6 If Simon wants to keep his friends he couldn't keep boring them with details of his celebrity obsession.

Pronunciation

Modal stress and meaning
Go to page 119.

VOCABULARY

Admiration

centre of attention
object of affection
addiction (addict [n], addicted [adj])
fascination (with)
worship
idol
stalking (stalker [n], stalk [v])
fixation (on)

Fame

be in the limelight
up-and-coming
has-been
follow (something) on
A-list
one to watch out for
disappear without a trace
keep a low profile

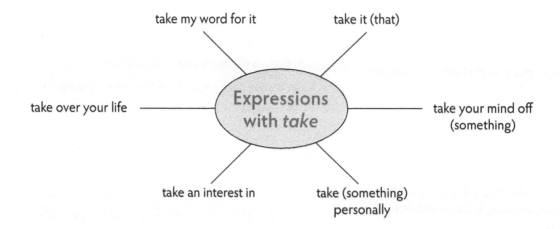

Key words in context

coverage	The TV **coverage** of the Olympics was great and they showed loads of different sports.
escalate	The police say that they expect the violence on the streets to **escalate** tonight and are sending more officers to deal with it.
extrovert	He's a real **extrovert** – he's always talking and smiling with people.
glamorous	She's very **glamorous**. Her hair is always perfect and she wears the latest fashions.
gleaming	Their car is brand new. Look at it **gleaming** in the sunshine.
instinct	The ability to swallow food without thinking is one of the many **instincts** we are born with.
luxurious	We had a really **luxurious** holiday – 1st class flights and a 5-star hotel.
make a scene	He **made** such **a scene** in the restaurant just because his soup was cold. It was so embarrassing.
public eye	If you want to be famous, you'll need to get used to being in the **public eye**.
reciprocated	Unfortunately my love for her was not **reciprocated** and she said 'no' when I asked her to marry me.

Admiration SB page 58

1 ★★ **Complete the sentences with the correct form of the words/phrases in the list.**

addiction | worship | idol | object of affection | fascination with | fixation on | stalk | centre of attention

1 Everywhere I go I bump into Tim. I think he might be _____ me.

2 Their dog is the _____ in their house. They talk to the dog more than each other.

3 I think I might be _____ to chocolate. I have to have 3 bars a day.

4 My younger brother has a _____ how things work. He loves taking old electronic devices apart.

5 The British seem to be _____ house prices. It's all they talk about!

6 Lady Gaga was my _____ when I was younger. I thought she was great.

7 Bobby likes to be the _____ and gets pretty upset when he thinks people are ignoring him.

8 I _____ my older sister when I was a kid and I still think she's the best.

Fame SB page 61

2 ★ **Match words in column A and B to write words and phrases.**

A

disappear | A-keep | follow | has-one to watch | be in up-and-

B

on Twitter the limelight a low profile | coming without a trace out for | list | been

3 ★★ **Complete the text with the correct form of the words and phrases from Exercise 2.**

Does anyone remember Ricky Stardust? Well I do. I remember his first appearance on TV in 1998. The presenter introduced him as an [1]_____ star and [2]_____ in the future.

Half a year later he was most certainly [3]_____. You couldn't pick up a teenage magazine without seeing his face on the cover. Although he wasn't what you might describe as an [4]_____ celebrity, he was popular with thousands of fans all over the country, though of course in those days you couldn't [5]_____ someone _____. You had to buy magazines to keep up to date with your idols.

I'm not really sure what went wrong. The future was looking really good for him but then he sort of [6]_____. One day he was everywhere, the next day he was nowhere. He was a [7]_____ almost overnight.

These days he [8]_____. In fact, it's almost impossible to find out anything about him. But I remember Ricky Stardust because he's my dad.

4 ★★★ **Think of a famous person for each question. Give a reason for your answer.**

Who …

1 really enjoys being in the limelight?

_____

2 is an up-and-coming star? _____

3 is a has-been? _____

4 do you (or someone you know) follow on Twitter?

_____

5 is an A-list star you really admire?

_____

6 is someone to watch out for? _____

7 likes to keep a low profile? _____

WordWise SB page 63

Expressions with *take*

5 ★★ **Match the sentence halves.**

1 You don't have to take my word for it – ☐

2 From that look on your face ☐

3 I know you're worried about your exams but ☐

4 I wasn't actually talking about you – ☐

5 It would be nice if Dad took an interest in my life – ☐

6 It's great that you've got a new hobby but ☐

a I take it that you don't like my new haircut.

b don't take everything so personally all the time.

c he has no idea what I'm up to half of the time.

d you need to find something to take you mind off them for a while.

e try not to let it take over your life.

f ask Mrs Page if you don't believe me.

READING

1 REMEMBER AND CHECK **Answer the questions. Then read the article on page 57 of the Student's Book again and check.**

1 Why might a visitor to Earth make wrong assumptions about our leaders?

2 What modern-day tradition is Queen Victoria responsible for?

3 What has made it easier for us to see the lifestyles of celebrities?

4 Why might celebrities be taking the place of 'family'?

5 What characteristics might a mild sufferer of CWS have?

6 What characteristics might a severe sufferer of CWS have?

2 **Read the newspaper article. What caused offence – a professional cyclist, a selfie or a comedian?**

3 **Read the article again and decide if the sentences are T (true), F (false) or DS (doesn't say).**

1 Marcel Kittel failed to finish the race in Dublin.

2 McCarthy asked Kittel if he could take a photo.

3 The Giro d'Italia that year involved more than one country.

4 McCarthy soon learned that most people didn't share his sense of humour over the incident.

5 Roche persuaded McCarthy to write an apology.

6 McCarthy was reluctant to apologise.

7 McCarthy sent his apology directly to Kittel.

8 Kittel was able to empathise with McCarthy.

4 **Choose one of the options and write a short paragraph.**

a Imagine you are McCarthy. Write your apology.

b Write a short text about a time you had to make an apology.

Think before you snap

Fans have always done crazy things to get up close and personal with their idols, but one Irish cycling fan may have just taken things a step too far. David McCarthy was watching the third stage of the Giro d'Italia as it passed through the streets of Dublin. He was standing at the finish line when the German cyclist Marcel Kittel collapsed in exhaustion in front of him having just won the race. McCarthy saw this as the perfect opportunity to run over and take a selfie with the overwhelmed cyclist, which he immediately posted on Instagram with the caption 'Kittel collapsed after the line today so instead of giving him a hand up I took a selfie.'

It was the end of the tour for Kittel, who had won the last two stages of the race. The following day he came down with a fever and had to withdraw before the race headed to Italy. However, this was far from the end of the story for David McCarthy, and it wasn't long before his post attracted large amounts of negative comments. It seemed that the general public were none too impressed with his selfish selfie.

Australian professional cyclist Cadel Evans called the photo 'more than inconsiderate' while local Irish cycling hero Nicholas Roche commented that it was 'not very respectful and definitely not very funny.' Other comments posted on his account were far less friendly. 'Pity there's no photo where Kittel actually punches him' one person wrote; 'Probably meant as funny. I find this quite disturbing,' wrote another.

What annoyed some people more was that McCarthy himself is a junior cyclist with ambitions, who should have appreciated the effort that Kittel had made to win the stage with virtually no help from his teammates. It was no surprise that he was suffering from exhaustion.

However, there is a happy end to the story. McCarthy soon realised that his actions had overstepped the mark and wrote an apology to the German rider in which he explained that he had never meant to cause so much offence and added that he had just got over-excited by the whole occasion. He said that he now realised that he had been completely wrong in his actions and offered a wholehearted apology to Kittel and anyone else he had offended.

The apology was forwarded on to Kittel, who seemed to be able to see the funny side. He responded to the young Irish fan about the lessons we learn in life, adding a story of his own about a time he was caught by his grandmother dangerously playing with fireworks. He also reminded McCarthy how brutal social media can be.

Hopefully McCarthy has learned his lesson and will think twice in the future about how and when he takes a selfie.

DEVELOPING WRITING

An essay

1 Read the essay and complete the sentence to sum up the writer's conclusion.

The writer would like to be famous as long as …

_____

2 Use the essay to complete the plan.

① Introduction
Talk about how there are _____
(keep this short)

② Pros
 • _____
 • 'power' e.g. – _____
 • _____ (most important)

③ Cons
 • _____
 • _____

④ My conclusion
 • _____

3 Look at the words in italics in the essay. What does each one refer to?

0 *some — people famous for a short time*
1 _____
2 _____
3 _____
4 _____
5 _____
6 _____
7 _____

4 You are going to write an essay about an aspect of celebrity life. Brainstorm some personality adjectives to describe what celebrities are like and the positive and negative aspects of being a celebrity.

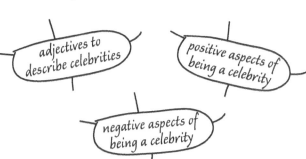

adjectives to describe celebrities

positive aspects of being a celebrity

negative aspects of being a celebrity

Would you want to be famous? Discuss the pros and cons of being a celebrity and give your reasons.

With the rise of the Internet and social media, more and more people are becoming famous. For ⁰*some*, the fame may last for only a few weeks before they disappear without a trace, ¹*others* might find themselves in the limelight for much longer. The question is; would you really want ²*it* at all?

Most people probably associate fame with wealth and, for many, this is one of the greatest attractions of being famous. But even more alluring than the money must be the power that having a high profile provides. Never having to worry about booking a table at the fanciest restaurants or getting tickets to the top sporting occasions, ³*these* are the sorts of luxury that fame can offer. Above all the greatest attraction of being famous is surely having the knowledge that you have achieved remarkable things and earned the respect of the public and your peers.

Of course, many people these days are becoming celebrities without really having to do anything particularly significant. In cases such as ⁴*these*, the attention never lasts long. But for ⁵*those* who do manage to maintain a good following for a long time, there are the problems of always being in the public eye. After a while ⁶*this* must get really tiring.

In conclusion, I would like to be famous for being the best at what I do. I would be recognised by others working in my field but not known to the majority of other people. ⁷*This* would mean I would have the respect of the people I also have admiration for, but my private life would remain my own.

5 Choose one of the ideas below and write an essay of 220–260 words.

A There should be laws to protect the privacy of celebrities.

B Reality TV shows should be banned.

CHECKLIST ✔

_____
_____
_____
_____

LISTENING

1 🔊 19 **Listen to the conversations and write the names *Stan*, *Shelley* or *Anna* under the photos of what they're talking about. There is one extra picture.**

1

2

3

4

2 🔊 19 **Listen again and choose the correct answers.**

Conversation 1

1 How many days in a row does Stan have band practice?

A 2   B 3   C 4

2 What does Stan promise to do with Lana at the weekend?

A He's going to let her choose.

B take her to a gig

C teach her guitar

Conversation 2

3 How many minutes does Shelley need to finish her game?

A 1   B 2   C 30

4 Which of these doesn't Dad mention?

A playing games

B watching videos

C surfing the Internet

Conversation 3

5 Why is Anna working so hard on her project?

A She hasn't got much time left to finish it.

B She's really interested in the subject.

C She wants to get a good result.

6 How is Anna related to Gill?

A She's Gill's little sister.

B She's Gill's big sister.

C They aren't actually related.

DIALOGUE

1 **Put the words in order to make lines from the conversations.**

1 got / do / Haven't / else / time / your / anything / you / with / to / ?

_____

2 do / all / seem / you / It's / ever / to / .

_____

3 I / this / got / for / haven't / now / time / .

_____

4 really / need / I / this / now / don't / .

_____

5 playing / on it, / watching / you're / not / If / videos / games / you're / .

_____

6 work / always / school / It's / .

_____

7 Gill. / me / Come / Give / on, / a / break / .

_____

8 spend / how / hate / homework / week / think / time / to / doing / much / I / you / each / .

_____

PHRASES FOR FLUENCY SB page 63

1 **Put the dialogue in the correct order.**

	JAMES	I've looked in my room and it's not there.
	JAMES	That's not true, Mum. I've got loads of other interests.
	JAMES	You might have told me this would turn into the computer moan. Not again!
1	JAMES	Have you seen my phone, Mum?
	JAMES	I don't know. Last week maybe.
	JAMES	Come on, Mum. It's not that bad.
	MUM	Actually it is. Just out of curiosity, when was the last time you tidied it?
	MUM	No, but might it be in your room by any chance?
	MUM	Yes, like playing on your phone. But I guess at least you won't be doing that for a while.
	MUM	I'm just saying it's all you ever seem to do.
	MUM	Fat chance you could find anything in your room, it's such a mess.
	MUM	More like last year. If you spent less time on your computer and more time tidying, for a change, you wouldn't keep losing things.

2 **Write a short dialogue of 8 to 10 lines between a parent and their son/daughter. Include at least two examples of complaining and two of responding to complaints.**

Reading and Use of English Part 7

Exam guide: gapped text

In Part 7 you will read an article with some missing paragraphs. You have to decide which of the missing paragraphs fits best in each space.

- Read through the main text first for gist, ignoring any gaps. Then read the gapped paragraphs.
- Return to the main text and read the paragraph before and after the first gap. What kind of information is missing? Have a look at the options again and choose which one contains the missing information.
- Then reread the paragraph before the gap, the missing paragraph you have chosen and the paragraph after the gap. Does it make sense? If not, either try another paragraph or move on to the next gap.

1   You are going to read an extract from a magazine article. Five paragraphs have been removed from the extract. Choose from the paragraphs A–F the one which fits each gap (1–5). There is one extra paragraph which you do not need to use.

How many Twitter followers do you need to get a hotel discount?

We all know how powerful social media is. It's no surprise, then, that one company has based its entire business model on harnessing the positive power of the Internet.

1 ☐

To unlock the discounts all you have to do is supply Hotelied with links to your social media profiles as well as any reward programmes you might have with hotels or airlines.

2 ☐

I asked three other social media users to test the site: a partner in a law firm (my friend Imogen); an influential travel writer (Paul Steele aka The Bald Hiker, who has more than 600,000 followers on Twitter); and my mum, who's a retired sheltered housing manager.

3 ☐

I'm offered two discounts: The Dream Downtown, a boutique hotel in Manhattan, is available for $460 (a 20% discount on the original price of $575); and the luxurious Gansevoort Park offers $491 (a 10% discount on the price available on travel websites).

4 ☐

More surprisingly, Imogen, who's the only one of us who might conceivably book into a pricey hotel in New York, isn't offered any discount either. Her travel history and hotel and airline reward scheme memberships don't seem to count for anything. Clearly she doesn't spend enough time on Facebook or Twitter.

5 ☐

It does seem that the website is pitched at someone who'd happily spend $500 a night on a hotel. If you're in that position then all you need is a LinkedIn page that says you have a cool job and as many Twitter followers as you can get your hands on.

A   To make it fair, we all search for hotel rooms in New York on Saturday 11th October (Hotelied are currently limited to four US cities – New York, LA, Miami and Palm Springs.)

B   The winner, perhaps unsurprisingly, turns out to be Paul Steele. He's offered the same deal as me at Dream Downtown but a more attractive $464 at Gansevoort Park. He says, however, that the offers 'start at expensive before the discount, and are still expensive [with the discount]. Not my style of travel'.

C   But just how popular do you have to be to get a discount? As a freelance food and travel journalist based in Alicante, I've only got 507 followers on Twitter but working in the media must be worth something, right? A quick and somewhat unscientific experiment reveals that the answer is probably not.

D   The problems start when I try to verify my Twitter account. It seems that Hotelied doesn't want to recognise my credentials for some reason. I have more luck when I link it with Facebook. It seems to like this account and I'm away.

E   New website, Hotelied is offering people with a big social media presence discounts on hotel stays. Using the strapline 'It pays to be you', it offers its members 'the opportunity to be rewarded for being themselves' by offering rates tailored to their social media profile.

F   Unsurprisingly, my mum isn't offered any discounts at all. This is probably because, although she does have a Twitter account, she's never tweeted.

CONSOLIDATION

LISTENING

1 🔊20 **Listen and complete the notes.**

Name: Tom Lackey
Current Age: [1]_____
Stunt: [2]_____
Departure: Castle Kennedy in [3]_____
Arrival: City of Derry Airport in [4]_____
Time taken: [5]_____
Previous world records:
Earlier in the same year: [6]_____
In 2005: [7]_____

2 🔊20 **Listen again and answer the questions with numbers.**

1 What year was the aircraft used built in? _____

2 How long has Mr Lackey been wing walking?

_____

3 How old was he when his wife died? _____

4 How much money has he raised for charity so far?

_____

5 When was he awarded the 'Pride of Britain'?

_____

6 How many times did he fly from the UK to France?

_____

7 How old was he when he wing walked on a plane as it looped-the-loop? _____

GRAMMAR

3 **Choose the correct option for each sentence.**

1 *Inspiring / Inspired* by the astronomy lecture, I went out and bought a telescope.

2 You *must / can't* be hungry. You haven't eaten all day.

3 I knew it was early because I heard birds *sing / singing*.

4 Having three brothers *can / may* be quite annoying at times. I know from experience.

5 *Cooking / Cooked* Asian food is the way I like to relax.

6 Dad *can't / won't* let me go to the game so you'll have to go without me.

7 I saw the man *fall / falling* off his bike and ran over to help him.

8 *Feeling / Felt* rather tired, I decided to have an early night.

VOCABULARY

4 **Complete with the missing prepositions.**

1 I like to follow my local politician _____ Twitter.

2 Whatever happened to Misty X? They just disappeared _____ a trace.

3 I get a real kick _____ of playing tennis. It's just the best sport.

4 Social media is great but you do need to be careful not to let it take _____ your life.

5 Have you heard of The Believers? They're certainly a band to watch _____ for.

6 Don't take my word _____ it. Ask Mr Thomas.

7 For crying _____ loud, Dave, that's the tenth time you've asked me the same question.

8 Why don't you watch a film to help take your mind _____ your exams for a while?

5 **Replace the words in italics with words from the list.**

has-been | peace and quiet | idol
stunts | a loudmouth | daredevil
centre of attention | stalker

1 There were lots of *dangerous action pieces* in the film.

_____

2 Don't tell her anything. She's *someone who always passes on secrets*.

_____

3 He hasn't made a successful film for more than 10 years. He's a *forgotten actor*.

_____

4 Everywhere she goes she wants to be the *focus of everything*.

_____

5 I love everything he does. He's my *star*.

_____

6 He's not scared to take risks. He's a *man who fears nothing*.

_____

7 I'm tired. I need a bit of *time to myself*.

_____

8 The actress complained to the police about the *person who was following her everywhere*.

_____

DIALOGUE

6 Complete the dialogue with the words in the list. There are two you won't use.

do | suppose | talk | point
accept | come | see | give

ED Mountain biking, mountain biking. It's all you ever ¹_____ about.

DI ²_____ on, Martin. It's my hobby. What's the problem?

ED But it's all you do. Haven't you got anything else to ³_____ with your time?

DI That's not true. I don't ⁴_____ that. I've got plenty of other hobbies.

ED Like what?

DI Well I'm in the girls' football team at school, I play the saxophone in the school band, I'm a member of the school eco council, I help out at the old people's home at the weekend. Do you want me to go on?

ED OK, ⁵_____ taken. But I do think you spend too much time on your mountain bike.

DI The way I ⁶_____ it is this. You think a mountain bike is too dangerous for a girl and you don't want to see me getting hurt. Well, Martin, I'm just not that type of girl and you've got to get used to it.

READING

7 Read the article and answer the questions.

Superfan's Dying Wish

Ever since he was eight years old, Daniel Fleetwood has been a huge Star Wars fan. When he was 21 he was featured in his local newspaper as he camped outside the cinema for days in order to be the first to buy a ticket for *Episode III: Revenge of the Sith*. Now, aged 32, Daniel has got to see the latest instalment of the series, *The Force Awakens*, weeks before anyone else.

Unfortunately this time the situation couldn't be more different. Daniel is suffering from cancer and back in July, he had been told by his doctors that he only had two months to live. The chances that he would make it to the opening of the film in December were slim. So family and friends started a huge public campaign to try and get Daniel to a private viewing before he passed away. Using the hash tag #forcefordaniel, thousands of people showed their support by sharing his story via Facebook and Reddit. The movement also gained support from actors in the film including Mark Hamill, who returns to the franchise to play Luke Skywalker, and John Boyega, who plays Finn, one of the heroes of the new film.

Daniel's dream for a private screening of the film came true when the film's director JJ Abrams phoned with the news that the Walt Disney studios had agreed to show Daniel the latest – albeit unfinished – version of the film.

This is not the first time that film makers have granted the dying wishes of their fans. Back in 2013, JJ Abrams also ensured that *Star Trek* super fan Daniel Craft got to see a version of his blockbuster *Star Trek Into Darkness*, five months before it was released. And in 2009, Walt Disney's subsidiary company Pixar flew a company executive with a DVD of the then unreleased animated film *Up* to the bedside of 10-year-old Colby Curtin, who was suffering from vascular cancer, so that she could watch the film she had been longing to watch ever since she first saw the trailer for it. She died the next day.

1 What evidence is given that Daniel is a 'superfan'?

_____

2 Why were Daniel's chances of seeing the film at its official opening in December 'slim'?

_____

3 Who launched the #forcefordaniel campaign and what was its aim?

_____

4 What famous names got involved in the campaign and how were they connected to the film?

_____

5 How is Daniel's story similar to that of Colby Curtin and Daniel Craft?

_____

WRITING

8 Write a letter from Daniel thanking JJ Abrams for allowing him to see a version of the film before its release and saying what it meant to you. Write about 180–200 words.

GRAMMAR

Substitution SB page 68

1 ★☆☆ **Circle the correct verbs to complete the mini-dialogues.**

1 A Do you think this class will help us to lose some weight?

   B I hope *so / it*.

2 A Are you finding the Insanity workout difficult?

   B Yes, a bit. There are some people who are really good at it and *those / that* who aren't.

3 A A lot of our friends used to go to Pilates classes.

   B A lot of people still *so / do*.

4 A I'd never heard of Zorbing before I came to this class.

   B *So / Neither* had we.

5 A I think the Tough Mudder will be really popular.

   B I reckon *so / one*.

6 A I have one goal, *those / that* of losing weight.

   B Me too.

2 ★★☆ **Complete the dialogue with the words in the list.**

those | so | the one | do | nor

ARNO   What's Surf Set? I've never heard of it.

BETH   ¹_____ have I. You're ²_____ who usually knows about all the latest fitness trends. Is it water aerobics classes? Helen tried one of ³_____. She said it was quite good.

ARNO   No, I don't think ⁴_____. I'll read out what it says. You stand on a mechanical surfboard that moves and shakes. You have to use your 'core balance' while doing a series of exercises such as squats and jumps.

BETH   I think it might be good.

ARNO   I ⁵_____ too.

3 ★★★ **Choose a true response to complete the mini-dialogues. Then justify your answers.**

I think so / don't think so | I do / Nor do I
I have / Neither have I | I reckon so / don't reckon so
People still do | So do I / I don't | So can I / I can't

0 A I think everybody should do at least half an hour of exercise a day.

   YOU *So do I. Then everybody would be much healthier.*

1 A I don't think sugary fizzy drinks are good for you.

   YOU _____

2 A Is it easy for people to lose weight?

   YOU _____

3 A I've never tried an ExerGame.

   YOU _____

4 A I reckon you'd be good at yoga.

   YOU _____

5 A I think Hula Hooping would be good fun.

   YOU _____

6 A I can stand on my head.

   YOU _____

4 ★★★ **Write sentences comparing the past and the present. Use the words in brackets. You can compare: cars, computers, video games, clothes, food.**

0 (that) *Music listened to today is much more fast-paced than that* listened to fifty years ago.

1 (that) _____ eaten a hundred years ago.

2 (those) _____ driven fifty years ago.

3 (that) _____ worn forty years ago.

4 (those) _____ used thirty years ago.

5 (those) _____ played twenty years ago.

Ellipsis SB page 69

5 ★ **Match the short sentences to the long sentences. Then complete the long sentences.**

0 _Would you like_ another coffee? | c |

1 _____ love one. | |

2 _____ fancy playing a game of tennis? | |

3 _____ time for a cup of tea? | |

4 _____ sorry but I can't stay. | |

5 _____ worry about it. | |

6 _____ want to listen to another track? | |

7 _____ seen you here before. | |

a Not seen you here before.
b Sorry, I can't stay.
c Another coffee?
d No worries.
e Love one.
f Time for a cup of tea?
g Fancy a game of tennis?
h Want to listen to another track?

6 ★★ **Write short versions of the sentences.**

0 That's great.
   Great.

1 I love your new haircut.

   _____

2 Would you like to have an ice cream?

   _____

3 Have you got any chocolate?

   _____

4 Have you seen Sam today?

   _____

5 It isn't a problem.

   _____

7 ★★ **Cross out the unnecessary words in the answers to the questions.**

1 A Where's Cathy?
  B I don't know.
2 A Does Max know the address?
  B I'm not sure.
3 A I've got a new ExerGame.
  B That's nice.
4 A How are you?
  B I'm not bad.
5 A Would you like an apple?
  B Yes, please. I would like an apple.
6 A Shall we stay and watch the next film?
  B No, I think we had better go home now.

8 ★★ **Circle the correct answer.**

1 A Have you seen any good films recently?
  B _A couple. / Got a couple._
2 A How do you feel?
  B _Great. / It's great._
3 A Jeremy has got into university.
  B _Interest. / Interesting._
4 A Have you ever been to a Pilates class?
  B _Not today. / Once._
5 A Would you like some more ice cream?
  B _Love some. / Love one._
6 A Would you like to come to a football match on Saturday?
  B _Love one. / Love to._

GET IT RIGHT!
Substitution

Learners often make mistakes when using _so_ or _either_ by omitting them or by using _it_ instead.

✓ _Do you think I'll pass the exam? I hope so._

✗ _Do you think I'll pass the exam? I hope._

Rewrite the sentences including _so_, _either_ or _neither_. Some of the sentences are incorrect and some can be shortened.

0 Emily is very fashionable – well, certainly more fashionable than me.
   Emily is very fashionable – well, certainly more so than me.

1 Rebecca thinks Kathryn needs to run greater distances in training if she's going to complete the marathon and she thinks it too.

   _____

2 Monica hasn't been to a fitness class in ages and Jo hasn't been to a fitness class.

   _____

3 My mum thinks that ripped jeans will soon go out of fashion and my dad certainly hopes it too!

   _____

4 Mark doesn't like the retro look and so doesn't Finn.

   _____

5 Smartphones have become a must-have and tablets have.

   _____

6 John is going to cut down on his sugar intake and George is going to cut down on his sugar intake.

   _____

VOCABULARY

Fads

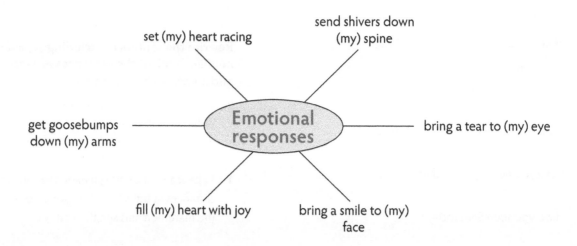

bang on trend

GO OUT OF FASHION

must-have

really in   a thing

short-lived   THE NEXT BEST THING

set (my) heart racing

send shivers down (my) spine

get goosebumps down (my) arms

Emotional responses

bring a tear to (my) eye

fill (my) heart with joy

bring a smile to (my) face

Key words in context

appealing	That piece of spinach cake doesn't look very **appealing**. I think it's the green colour.
aspire	He **aspires** to be a poet and I think he will be one day. He's very talented.
contradiction	You want to go on a diet but you hate seeing pictures of thin models in fashion magazines. Isn't that a **contradiction**?
craze	Everyone's got hair extensions at the moment but I don't think this **craze** will last.
dawn on	I didn't understand what the poem meant at first. Then it suddenly **dawned on** me. It was a poem about survival.
health threat	The amount of sugar and caffeine in energy drinks poses a serious **health threat**. It can lead to diabetes and heart problems.
infuriating	Sometimes the traffic is **infuriating**. I hate it when we're late for a match because we're stuck in traffic.
last long	This protective case is made from a very cheap plastic. I don't think it will **last long**. It will break soon.
unattainable	My mum says no goal is **unattainable**. You can do or be anything if you work hard.

Fads `SB page 68`

1 ★   Match the words to complete the expressions.

1	go out	a	lived
2	bang	b	thing
3	really	c	have
4	short-	d	of fashion
5	a	e	in
6	must-	f	best thing
7	the next	g	on trend

2 ★★   Circle the correct words to complete the statements about fashion.

Fashion in 1990s America and Britain

1 In the late 1980s and the early 1990s bright coloured tops and leg warmers were *bang on trend / short-lived*.

2 Mid 1992 'grunge' fashion became popular and fingerless gloves and ripped jeans were *out of fashion / really in* for men.

3 Aviator-style sunglasses, popularised by the rock star Freddie Mercury, were the *really in / must-have* fashion accessory.

4 Fashions in trousers were often *short-lived / the next best thing* but jeans survived the decade and will do for many more.

5 In the late 1990s, there was a 1970s revival and platform shoes were fashionable. If you didn't have a pair of platform shoes, a pair of knee-high boots were *the next best thing / out of fashion*.

6 In 1995 baggy jeans, tracksuits and 'bomber' jackets were *a thing / short-lived*.

7 By 2000, baggy jeans *were the next best thing / had gone out of fashion*. It wasn't trendy to wear them any more.

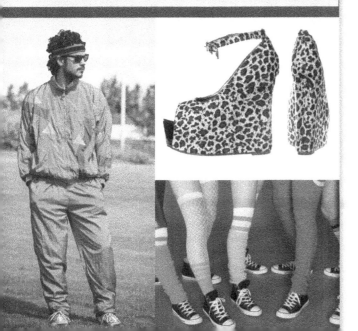

Emotional responses `SB page 71`

3 ★★   Read the clues and complete the puzzle with the words missing from the expressions. Find the mystery word.

```
1 [ ][ ][ ][ ][ ][ ][ ]
2 [ ][ ][ ][ ][ ][ ][ ]
        [P]
        [P]
3     [ ][P][ ][ ][ ]
        [N]
4   [ ][N][ ][ ][ ]
      5 [ ][ ][ ][ ][ ]
6 [ ][ ][ ][ ][ ][ ][ ][ ][ ]
```

1 It sends … down my spine.
2 It sets my heart … .
3 It … my heart with joy.
4 It brings a … to my eye.
5 It brings a … to my face.
6 I get … down my arms.

   The mystery word is _____ .

4 ★★   Complete the dialogues with expressions from Exercise 3 and your own ideas.

1 A Do you have a favourite song or piece of music?

   B I love _____ (name of song/music). It _____ when I hear the opening chords.

2 A Do you know any sad songs?

   B Yes, I do. _____ (name of song). It _____ whenever I listen to it.

3 A Where would you say is the place you feel happiest?

   B _____ (name of a place). It _____ whenever I think of it.

4 A Have you ever heard _____ (name of a singer) sing?

   B Yes, I have. He/She has such an amazing voice. I _____ whenever I listen to him/her sing.

5 A Can you think of anything scary or anything that gives you a thrill?

   B _____ .

6 A What makes you smile?

   B When I see _____ (name of person/pet). _____ .

READING

1 REMEMBER AND CHECK Mark the sentences T (true) or F (false). Then read the article on page 67 of the Student's Book again and check.

The writer claims …

1 keeping fit these days is more complicated than it was in the past. ☐

2 exercise was important to the Ancient Greeks for them to be ready to go to war. ☐

3 technology plays a bigger part in exercise these days. ☐

4 you can exercise while travelling to work with an exergame. ☐

5 today's world is not very different to that of the Ancient Greeks. ☐

6 we no longer have the same need to exercise as in the past. ☐

2 Read the article quickly and find out what each of these toxins was used in.

lead | arsenic | deadly nightshade | DNP

3 Read the article again. Then write the questions for these answers.

1 _____ ?

Queen Elizabeth I.

2 _____ ?

Grey hair, very dry skin, stomachaches, swollen brains, and finally a very painful death.

3 _____ ?

Because the red blood cells had been destroyed.

4 _____ ?

It is one of the most poisonous plants.

5 _____ ?

She drove herself.

6 _____ ?

People are drawn by the cheap prices and claims of success.

Pronunciation

Connected speech feature: assimilation

Go to page 120. 🔊

THE PRICE OF BEAUTY

Over the centuries some very dangerous products have been used to follow fashions of the time.

The Secret of a Good Complexion
TO ALL WOMEN WHO DESIRE BEAUTY.
Until further notice we will send you a 30-day daily treatment of Dr. Campbell's Safe Arsenic Complexion Wafers and a 30-day daily treatment of Fould's Medicated Arsenic Soap FOR ONE DOLLAR.
These world-famous preparations are a never failing remedy for bad blood, pimples, freckles, blackheads, moth patches, liver spots, acne, redness of face or nose, wrinkles, dark rings under the eyes, and all other blemishes, whether on the face, neck, arms or body. They brighten and beautify the complexion as no other remedies on earth can, and they do it in a very short time. They impart to the complexion the most exquisite fairness, make the skin clear, soft and velvety. Until further notice we will send you the wafers and soap as stated above for $1.00. After this offer is withdrawn the price will be $1.00 for the wafers and 50c. for the soap. Address or call on:
H. B. FOULD, Dept. A, 214 Sixth Ave., New York.
Sold by Druggists Everywhere.

Using lead in make-up

Queen Elizabeth I of England started the fashion for pale skin. In her time, it was considered beautiful to have a very white face, and she used a lead face powder to achieve this look. Lead powder was easy to make and it was cheap, so men and women would put thick layers of it onto their faces every day. This achieved the pale smooth look they wanted, but sadly, the lead in the powder was slowly poisoning them. Symptoms included grey hair, very dry skin, stomachaches, swollen brains, and finally a very painful death.

Arsenic pills and soaps

The use of the poison arsenic for losing weight and improving your skin seems to have begun in the 1850s. James F. W. Johnston, a Scottish agricultural chemist, made arsenic pills famous after he wrote an article about them in his book *The Chemistry of Common Life*, which was first published in 1855. After this, adverts began to appear for arsenic pills and soaps.

The pills made the skin pale by destroying red blood cells. In July 1880, there was an article in an American newspaper, the *Indianapolis Sentinel*, about a young lady who had gradually lost her sight as a result of taking arsenic pills. People also died taking the pills. In 1911, 18-year-old Hildegarde Walton of St Louis in America died after taking several boxes of pills to clear up the spots on her face.

Deadly nightshade eye drops

The poisonous plant, deadly nightshade, or Belladonna, was used in eye drops by women from Roman times until the late 19th century. It made the eyes look more attractive. Unfortunately, deadly nightshade is one of the most poisonous plants on the planet. Using these eye drops caused sight problems and blindness. It also caused other serious health problems, and eventually death.

Dangerous diet pills today

Eloise Aimee Parry, a 21-year-old university student in the UK, bought some slimming pills on the Internet. When she started to feel unwell, she drove herself to hospital. She told the doctors what she had taken. The pills contained a dangerous ingredient, DNP. Eloise tragically died.

We now live in the 21st century and our medical knowledge has improved, but have things changed? It would seem not. The price some people are willing to pay for beauty, it seems, is still their lives. Attracted by cheap prices and claims of success, many people are buying unregulated and dangerous health and beauty products over the Internet and unfortunately paying for them with their lives. Be aware of the dangers.

4 Write a dialogue of 8 to 10 lines between two friends.

Friend A wants to buy a 'miracle cure' on the Internet.
Friend B wants to convince him/her of the dangers and stop him/her from buying it.

DEVELOPING WRITING

A letter of complaint

1   Read the letter of complaint about Vita-Hair shampoo and conditioner. Find and underline the three sentences that express too much anger or are inappropriate.

The Manager
Revitalise Hair & Beauty Products
PO Box 1065
London
UK

Dear Sir/Madam,

I am writing to you to complain about one of your products, Vita-Hair shampoo and conditioner, which I recently purchased from your website. I feel that the language used in the advertisement for the product is very misleading.

The advertisement claims that it is 'a revolutionary new product' that after just one use will give me 'fuller thicker hair'. That's rubbish! I have been using Vita-Hair for three months now and I haven't noticed any difference in the thickness of my hair.

Secondly, the advertisement asks, 'Have you always dreamed of having shiny healthy hair?' and then it promises, 'Vita-Hair will give you that dream hair.' In fact, my friends and family say my hair has become dull and lifeless. My mum even asked me if I was ill. This is the worst shampoo I've ever tried.

Finally, according to the advertisement there are only natural oils in the shampoo and conditioner. After receiving the product in the post, I checked the list of ingredients on the back of the bottles, and I found that there are several chemicals in the shampoo and conditioner. How can you lie to people like that?

The product was on offer for a limited length of time so unfortunately I bought it. I feel that your advertisement for the product is misleading and I would like a refund.

Please let me know as soon as possible what you propose to do.

Yours faithfully,

Sally Jones

2   Complete the reasons Sally gives for her complaint.

1   The advert claims to _____

_____

After 3 months, Sally _____

2   The advert promises to _____

_____

The shampoo makes _____

3   The advert says that _____

_____

The shampoo contains _____

3   Now write a letter of complaint about a product you have recently bought. Write 220–260 words.

Ideas: an electronic item | a game
a beauty product | an exercise DVD

Writing tip: a letter of complaint

- Express your unhappiness with the product but be polite and reasonable.
- Include language of persuasion. Quote what the advertisement said.
- Begin a new paragraph for each main point. Be concise.
- State clearly what you would like to be done.

CHECKLIST ✔

LISTENING

1 🔊 **23** Alice and Nicole are at a Health and Beauty Fair. Which products do the words below describe? Listen and write (T) for toothpaste or (S) for shampoo.

organic ☐   green tea ☐

almond oil ☐   smells amazing ☐

protects and cleans ☐   nice packaging ☐

2 🔊 **23** Listen again and complete these parts of the conversation.

1 ASSIST 1 Would you like to try one of our ¹_____ toothpastes?

    ALICE Maybe.

    ASSIST 1 ²_____ this organic green tea toothpaste. It doesn't contain any artificial colours or harsh preservatives, and it protects, cleans and whitens your teeth.

2 NICOLE The big question for me is does it *really* whiten your teeth?

    ASSIST 1 ³_____ white teeth is important to you and so our organic toothpastes do all contain a tooth whitening ingredient. However, we do have an even more effective and established tooth whitening product which has had excellent results. ⁴_____ it's whitened their teeth. It's £99 for the first treatment.

3 ASSIST 2 I'm sure you'll like what's in the bottles too. ⁵_____ having really shiny, healthy hair?

    ALICE Don't I already?

    ASSIST 2 Yes, well ... maybe I should have said shinier and healthier. ⁶_____ shinier, healthier hair. So would you say you have dry hair, or normal?

    NICOLE I'd say my hair is generally quite dry.

    ALICE Me too. What's special about your range?

    ASSIST 2 We use ⁷_____ of plant extracts and oils.

4 NICOLE How much is it then?

    ASSIST 2 It's £9.99. ⁸_____. It's just for this fair.

DIALOGUE

1 Complete the advertising speeches with the phrases in the list.

strongly recommend | revolutionary new
This brand new | We understand that
Imagine | This offer is limited
one million people worldwide
Have you always dreamt of

RUNNING THE DREAM

¹_____ running a marathon? Then let us help you to make your dream come true. ²_____ training to run 42.19 km isn't easy and we ³_____ that you pay a visit to your doctor before you start training. Once you have the go-ahead from your doctor, you can ease your way into training with a few walks and gentle jogs. Develop your training routine at a natural and healthy pace.

All eyes on you

Make sure all eyes are on you with our fantastic selection of sunglasses at amazingly low prices. Whatever your style, we've got just the sunglasses for you. Last year, ⁴_____ chose to wear our sunglasses. All our sunglasses offer a high level of UV protection as well as being stylish. Try our dark blue retro square sunglasses for only £59.99.

Hurry! ⁵_____ and will end on Friday.

Cycle in comfort and style

The Trumpington is a ⁶_____ design for bikes. It's made of light-weight metal and has a small motor to help you on those steep hills. ⁷_____ design makes the bike a lot more comfortable to ride. ⁸_____ being able to ride for hours without feeling at all tired.

2 Write an advertising speech recommending a product. Use phrases from Exercise 1.

Ideas: a new beauty product | a sugar-free drink
some new exercise equipment | an ExerGame

CAMBRIDGE ENGLISH: Advanced

Reading and Use of English part 4

Exam guide: key word transformations

In part 4 of the exam, there are six questions. Each question has a sentence, followed by a key word and a gapped sentence. You must complete the gaps with three to six words, including the key word given, so that the second sentence has the same meaning as the first.

- Look carefully at the structure of the original sentence.
- Check the tense.
- Look at the words around the gap in the second sentence. Ask yourself questions: What verbs go with the preposition or what prepositions go with the word? Is it followed by an infinitive or a gerund?
- To practise for the test, always check the synonyms of words and expressions you look up in your dictionary.

1 For questions 1–6, complete the second sentence so that it has a similar meaning to the first sentence, using the word given. Do not change the word given. You must use between three and six words, including the word given. Here is an example (0).

0 In Lord Byron's day, poets were expected to be pale and thin, so Lord Byron persistently went on diets to achieve the romantic image.

INSIST

In Lord Byron's day, poets were expected to be pale and thin so Lord Byron _____*insisted on dieting*_____ to achieve the romantic image.

1 He wasn't naturally thin. He followed an extremely strict diet because he didn't want to put on weight.

FAT

He wasn't naturally thin. Afraid _____ an extremely strict diet.

2 Byron only ate a thin slice of bread and a cup of tea for breakfast.

EXCEPT

Byron _____ a thin slice of bread and a cup of tea for breakfast.

3 By 1822, he had starved himself into a poor state of health.

DUE

The poor state of health he was in by 1822 _____ himself.

4 He was well aware that poor diet led to ill health.

CAUSE

He knew that many illnesses _____ eating well.

5 In 1806, he weighed 81 kg and by 1811, he weighed just 57 kg.

LOT

Between 1806 and 1811, Lord Byron _____ weight.

6 Lord Byron had a huge cultural influence on the youth of the day so his dieting had a bad effect on young people.

EXAMPLE

Lord Byron's dieting _____ young people of the day.

GRAMMAR

Relative clauses with determiners and prepositions SB page 76

1 ★★☆ **Match the pictures to the sentences. Then circle the correct options in the sentences.**

 A
 B
 C
 D
 E
 F

These are photographs of our family from my grandmother's photo album.

1 The tall fat man in this picture is my grandfather, *compared to which / compared to whom* my father beside him is quite thin, really.

2 There are five children in this photo, *all of which / all of whom* are my cousins.

3 There are several older women in this photo, *one of whom / some of whom* are my grandmother's aunts.

4 Here's my grandfather's little old car, *compared to which / compared to whom* our modern car is huge.

5 Here's a picture of several old dolls, *one of which / some of which* was my grandmother's when she was a child.

6 The woman sitting in this picture is holding two babies, *one of whom / both of whom* is me!

2 ★★☆ **Complete the sentences with a phrase in the list. Use each phrase once only.**

one of which | compared to which | in which case
none of whom | most of which | both of which

1 My sister speaks Spanish and Portuguese, _____ I find very difficult.

2 My father lent me some books, _____ is in German, so I can't read it.

3 Ed went to Thailand with his friends, _____ speak Thai, so they had difficulty getting around.

4 Tammy is studying Hungarian, _____ English is really very simple.

5 Fred might go and work in Hong Kong, _____ he will have to learn some Chinese.

6 My dad speaks five languages, _____ are from his home country, India.

3 ★★★ **Complete the sentences with phrases with a determiner from list A, *whom* or *which* and a phrase from list B. Use each phrase once only.**

A

most of | many of | most of | none of | one of
none of | some of

B

said they could come. | plays basketball professionally.
agreed with the proposal, but others didn't.
ever got married. | she bought on the Internet.
won the prize. | are free, but you have to pay for most.

1 Jason is really disappointed. He bought ten lottery tickets, _____

2 Dani is very happy. She invited a lot of friends, _____

3 Sam has a lot of very tall cousins, _____

4 My grandmother lived with her six sisters, _____

5 Sue has dozens of model frogs, _____

6 200 people answered the survey, _____

7 There are some interesting places to visit in the city, _____

however / wherever / whatever, etc.

SB page 77

4 ★★ **Complete the gaps with** *however, wherever, whenever, whoever* **or** *whatever*.

1 _____ you go in the world, English can be useful.

2 Brazilian people are very kind. _____ badly you speak Portuguese, they're happy you're making the effort.

3 My brother and I invented a secret language which we used _____ we didn't want our parents to understand us.

4 We can speak English or French, _____ you're most comfortable with.

5 _____ you do, don't comment on her spelling. She knows it isn't good.

6 Three dictionaries as prizes will be awarded to _____ gets the most correct answers.

7 Pierre turns on the subtitles _____ a film is in English.

8 _____ long you study a language, there is always more to learn.

5 ★★ **Complete the gaps with a** *wh-* **word or an** *-ever* **word. Always use the** *-ever* **form when it is possible.**

− □ ✕

1 It was June _____ I visited the island.

2 The people in the village _____ I stayed were really nice to me.

3 _____ I went on the island everybody was friendly.

4 Fortunately there were a lot of people _____ spoke English.

5 The hostel provided me with _____ I wanted – guidebooks, maps, etc. Anything!

6 There were so many places to visit on the island that I had some difficulty deciding _____ to do first.

7 The beaches are at their best in the morning, when they're quiet, but they're beautiful _____ you go there.

8 The people are proud of their history. _____ I spoke to, they knew a lot.

---

6 ★★★ **Rewrite the extract from a letter, replacing the underlined phrases with phrases including an** *-ever* **word.**

... ¹<u>It doesn't matter what</u> you decide to do with your life, you need to have languages behind you. ²<u>It's not important where</u> you go, you will have to communicate with people. When I was at school, ³<u>any and every person who</u> was studying sciences also had to study a language. I know I found it very helpful ⁴<u>at any time</u> I was in France. I could contribute to a conversation, ⁵<u>it didn't matter what</u> it was about. So try to learn a language – or two, or three! ⁶<u>It doesn't matter how</u> difficult it seems at the time, your efforts will be rewarded. ⁷<u>It's not important where</u> you study, how much you learn depends on you.

So, work hard, have fun and be successful! And good luck – Bonne chance! Buena suerte! Viel Gluck! zhù nǐ háoyùn! In bocca al lupo!

GET IT RIGHT!

however / wherever / whatever, etc.

Learners often omit *-ever* **from** *whatever, however,* **etc. sentences.**

✓ ***Whichever*** *way I choose to go always seems to be the wrong way!*

✗ ~~Which~~ *way I choose to go always seems to be the wrong way!*

Tick the sentences which are correct and rewrite the incorrect ones.

1 It's important to who's receiving it. ☐

_____

2 I didn't quite get what he said but what he did say I'm not interested. ☐

_____

3 Who said that my accent was too strong to understand? ☐

_____

4 Whatever I do it always seems to be wrong! ☐

_____

5 I'm going to try to learn either Japanese or Chinese – I'll choose which course is cheaper. ☐

_____

6 How fluent you may be there will always be someone who doesn't follow you. ☐

_____

VOCABULARY

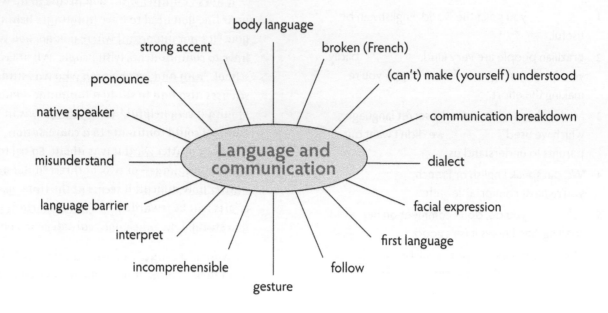

Language and communication

- body language
- strong accent
- pronounce
- native speaker
- misunderstand
- language barrier
- interpret
- incomprehensible
- gesture
- broken (French)
- (can't) make (yourself) understood
- communication breakdown
- dialect
- facial expression
- first language
- follow

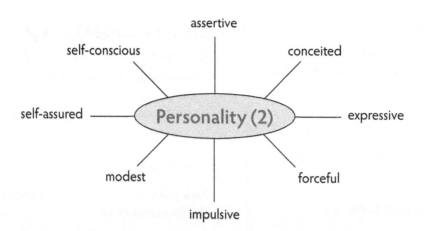

Personality (2)

- assertive
- self-conscious
- conceited
- self-assured
- expressive
- modest
- forceful
- impulsive

Key words in context

anticipate	I was late because I hadn't **anticipated** traffic jams at that time of day.
bilingual	She was born and raised in France but spoke English at home with her mother, so she's **bilingual**.
countless	I've heard that song **countless** times on the radio.
elicit	We're doing a survey to **elicit** information about people's eating habits.
engage in	He's really boring – try not to **engage in** a conversation with him!
exclusively	These cheap tickets are available **exclusively** to students.
fundamental	Having good pronunciation is **fundamental** to being understood in another language.
illustration	In most children's books, the story is accompanied by **illustrations**.
inherent	There are many **inherent** dangers in sports like rock climbing.
proficient	He practised hard for several months and became a **proficient** guitar player.
trait	I think her sense of humour is her best personality **trait**.
verbal	We didn't put it in writing – it was just a **verbal** agreement.

Language and communication
SB page 76

1 ★   **Circle the correct options.**

1   You can communicate a lot using *face / facial* expressions.

2   Someone who has spoken a certain language since they were born is a *native / first* speaker.

3   A movement you make with your hand(s) is a *gesture / body language*.

4   They use different words in that part of the country – it's a very different *dialect / barrier*.

5   He spoke so fast that he was *incomprehensible / broken*.

6   Some sounds in another language can be hard to *accent / pronounce*.

7   We misunderstood each other totally – it was a complete communication *breakdown / barrier*.

8   I like listening to French people speaking English – I think their *dialect / accent* is wonderful!

9   The language of the country you are born in is usually your *communication / first* language.

10 Your body *expression / language* tells people a lot about what you're really thinking.

2 ★★   **Complete the sentences with a word or phrase from the Word list (language and communication) on page 74.**

1   I couldn't understand a word of what she was saying – it was completely _____ to me.

2   What's the _____ of people who are born in Quebec – French or English?

3   I didn't mean that. She completely _____ me.

4   I knew immediately where he was from because he spoke with a very _____.

5   Sometimes, if you can't speak the language, a _____ with your hands will help.

6   However hard I tried, I couldn't _____ understood.

7   Her Spanish is so good that lots of people think she's a _____ – but in fact she's German.

8   It's hard to _____ people from that area because they pronounce words in a very different way.

9   They just stopped talking or listening to each other – it was a total _____.

10 I could tell she wasn't happy to see me – her _____ made it very clear, for example, when she crossed her arms.

Personality (2)   SB page 79

3 ★   **Match the words and the definitions.**

1 forceful ☐	5 modest ☐
2 self-assured ☐	6 expressive ☐
3 assertive ☐	7 self-conscious ☐
4 conceited ☐	8 impulsive ☐

a   stating your opinions strongly and demanding action or answers

b   not saying much about yourself or your abilities or achievements

c   having confidence in your own abilities

d   not afraid to say what you want or believe

e   showing what you think or feel

f   being too proud of yourself or your actions

g   nervous or uncomfortable because you're worried about what others think about you

h   suddenly deciding to do something and not thinking much about the result

4 ★★   **Write an adjective to describe each of these people.**

0   'Do you think this shirt looks alright? Is it the wrong colour for me?'   *self-conscious*

1   'Winning the Championship wasn't a big deal. I think I just got lucky.'   _____

2   'Hey! Let's not go to the cinema tonight – let's just get on a train and go somewhere, anywhere!'   _____

3   'Well, I'm sorry but I really disagree with you about that.'   _____

4   'I think I'll be OK in the interview – I'll be able to answer their questions, I reckon.'   _____

5   'His words and gestures make it easy to understand how he's feeling.'   _____

6   'Well you made a mistake and you have to do something about it – now!'   _____

7   'There's no doubt about it – I'm by far the most intelligent person in this school!'   _____

5 ★★★   **Choose three of the adjectives in the list. For each one, think of a person you know who can be described using that adjective. Write a short sentence to say why.**

assertive | conceited | expressive | forceful
impulsive | modest | self-assured | self-conscious

0   *My friend Sam is very impulsive. If he sees something he wants, he buys it right away.*

1   _____

2   _____

3   _____

READING

1 REMEMBER AND CHECK **Mark the sentences T (true), F (false) or DS (doesn't say). Then read the article on page 75 of the Student's Book again and check.**

1 Navajo is a language that is not written down. ▢

2 The only difficult thing about the Navajo language is the pronunciation. ▢

3 The Japanese had broken twenty American codes. ▢

4 The idea to create a code based on Navajo came from Chester Nez. ▢

5 A problem was the lack of words in Navajo for modern things. ▢

6 The Navajo word for 'turtle' was used to describe a kind of plane. ▢

7 None of the Navajo code-talkers were killed in the war. ▢

8 After the war, the code-talkers wanted to talk about their work. ▢

2 **Read the article quickly and find out …**

1 where this man works, and who for. _____

2 why he started learning languages. _____

3 which languages he doesn't speak. _____

3 **Put the sentences into the correct spaces in the article. There is one sentence you won't use.**

1 Nor was it his intelligence, which won him membership in the high-IQ society Mensa International.

2 Language is like love.

3 He didn't play football, and most school subjects bored him.

4 So Ikonomou kept up his travels through the languages and cultures of the world and continues to do so to this day.

5 Ikonomou is the best of them all.

6 With each visit, he learned more of the language.

7 He's never asked them of himself.

8 For 18 years, he was a strict vegetarian and lived by Hindu rules.

4 **Write three questions that you would ask Ikonomou if you met him. Then write what you think his answers might be.**

⊖ ▢ ⊗

The man who speaks 32 languages

Inside a grey office building in Brussels, Ioannis Ikonomou's workload is marked in different colours on his computer screen, the 49-year-old Greek translator [has received] three special requests: The EU Commission urgently needs translations of confidential documents from Hebrew, Chinese and Azerbaijani. Very few of the EU's 2,500 translators can handle that. **A** ▢ He speaks 32 languages virtually fluently, including a pair of dead languages. What his brain has managed to achieve is perhaps unique on the planet. How can a human being learn so many languages? And how does he live with that?

Ikonomou regards questions like that as 'funny'. **B** ▢ [...] He says his career developed out of curiosity. 'That's a keyword for my life.' [...]

He learned English at age five, German at seven ('Frau Rosi, a German lady on Crete, taught me'), Italian when he was barely 10 ('a school friend started to take it, and I wanted to be better than he was'), Russian at 13 ('I loved Dostoyevsky'), East African Swahili at 14 ('just for fun') and Turkish at 16. [...]

But it wasn't just his curiosity that turned Ikonomou into a language nut. **C** ▢ 'My friends all listened to the same Greek songs and ate souvlaki,' he says. 'But I wanted to get away from souvlaki, from my culture, from my roots. I was the opposite of Odysseus.' **D** ▢

[...] 'The rules of a language are only the beginning for me,' he says. 'I want to understand everything — the food, the music, the religion, the traumas of a people.' Then he took a giant step: Ikonomou suddenly became fascinated by India, and studied Urdu, Hindi and Sanskrit. **E** ▢

[...] Ikonomou speaks 21 of the total of 24 official EU languages. 'I forgot my Lithuanian, and I didn't have time for Gaelic or Maltese.' He understands not only modern languages, but also various old ones — Latin, of course, but also Old English, Mayan, Old Irish and Old Iranian.

'**F** ▢,' he says. 'When you really fall in love with someone you also want to know their whole story, meet their parents, visit their old schools. A language is not just the present for me but also the past.' [...]

Ikonomou's work requires him to translate primarily official documents, but he listens to worldwide chats, Internet TV, radio on his iPod in the mornings and evenings on the way to and from work, always in different languages. Lately he's been keeping up with the news in Chinese. [...]

'Chinese is my favourite language,' he says. 'It's completely different, the Mount Everest for Europeans.' He's been to China a few times. **G** ▢ The costs are borne by the Commission, mostly.

There are some countries whose languages he speaks that Ikonomou has never visited, including Ethiopia and the Congo. 'I just don't have the time.'

Writing up data from a graph

1 Look at the graph and read the text. Answer the questions.

1 Number the reasons in the order in which the writer discusses them.

2 Which reasons does the writer make a comment about?

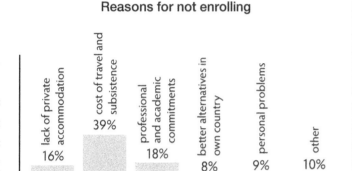

Reasons for not enrolling

- lack of private accommodation — 16%
- cost of travel and subsistence — 39%
- professional and academic commitments — 18%
- better alternatives in own country — 8%
- personal problems — 9%
- other — 10%

A school that offers courses in English decided to do a survey. They wanted to find out why people who contacted them about courses decided not to enrol.

Survey results

We conducted a survey of people who had contacted us about our courses but decided not to enrol. We wanted to find out more about the reasons for their decision. The results can be found in the bar chart above.

As can be seen, the <u>most significant factor</u> was how much it costs to travel to our country, <u>coupled with</u> the cost of living while they're here. Recent changes in exchange rates <u>account for</u> a lot of this concern, and <u>thus</u> we cannot necessarily <u>infer</u> that our fees are too high.

18% of respondents stated that a change to their work or college/university commitments meant that they were unable to take up the course they had hoped to enrol in.

One factor <u>worth noting</u> is that the decision of 16% of respondents not to enrol with us is <u>down to</u> the fact that we can only offer accommodation with local families – adult customers <u>in particular</u> stated that they wished to have private accommodation of some kind.

Other motives for not enrolling include personal problems (e.g. illness), as well as the discovery of alternative courses in the respondent's own country which they felt were at least as suitable, if not more so.

Finally, 10% of respondents selected 'other reasons', but none of them stated what those reasons were.

2 Find an underlined word or expression in the text which means …

1 a result of _____

2 are the reason for _____

3 come to the conclusion _____

4 especially _____

5 interesting enough to mention _____

6 most important reason _____

7 so _____

8 together with _____

3 You are going to write up the results of another survey that the school undertook to find out why students enrolled for a second term. Look at the graph showing the results and answer the questions.

In which order do you think you will write about them? Which ones are you going to explore in more detail? Number them in order and make brief notes.

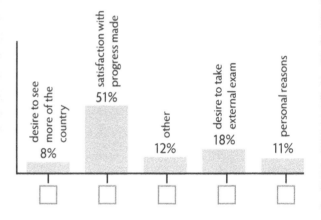

Reasons for enrolling for a second term

- desire to see more of the country — 8%
- satisfaction with progress made — 51%
- other — 12%
- desire to take external exam — 18%
- personal reasons — 11%

4 Write up the results in 200–220 words.

- Include an introduction.
- Discuss the reasons in the order you decided in Exercise 3.
- Use the text in Exercise 1 to help you.
- Use as many of the expressions in Exercise 2 as you can.

CHECKLIST ✔

LISTENING

1 🔊 24 **Listen to Greg talk about an experience he had in France. Answer the questions.**

1 Which picture shows the man in the story?

2 Which picture shows the old woman in the story?

3 Which picture shows the end of the story?

2 🔊 24 **Listen again. Correct the false information in each statement.**

1 The man tells a story about something that happened recently.
No, _____

2 He was going to visit relatives in Toulouse.
No, _____

3 The old woman was sitting in a chair and reading.
No, _____

4 The man's French was very good.
No, _____

5 He gestured to show the woman that he was foreign.
No, _____

6 He showed her the name 'Rue du Bac' on a map.
No, _____

7 The woman told him where Rue du Bac was.
No, _____

8 Rue du Bac was on the other side of the city.
No, _____

DIALOGUE

1 **Complete the mini-dialogues with the words/phrases in the list.**

didn't get | don't follow | familiar with
didn't catch | don't see | lost me

1 A It's very noisy in here, isn't it?
   B What? Sorry – I _____ that. Can you say it again?

2 A So, I decided not to do any more work on it, it was a thankless task.
   B 'Thankless task'? I'm not _____ that expression. Could you explain, please?

3 A So, in cricket, when a player is out, he goes back in and another player comes out to go in.
   B I'm sorry, you've _____ completely. What does that all mean?

4 A I'm sorry but I just _____ your argument at all.
   B OK, let me try to explain it another way.

5 A It's an interesting idea, but hard to understand.
   B That's right. To be honest, I _____ what he means at all.

6 A Wasn't that a great joke that she told?
   B Well, to be honest, I _____ it. That's why I didn't laugh much.

2 **Imagine you are at a party where the music is very loud. Someone is trying to tell you something in English but it's hard to hear and the person is using unusual vocabulary.**

Write a dialogue in 8–10 lines.

_____
_____
_____
_____
_____
_____
_____
_____

Pronunciation
Stress in multi-syllable words
Go to page 120.

Reading and Use of English part 6

Exam guide: cross-text multiple matching

In this part of the exam, you have to read four texts (A–D) on the same topic. Then you see four statements or questions, and you have to match them to the texts.

- Read all the texts first, before you read the statements/questions.
- Pay attention to what is similar or different in each text.
- Read the statements/questions and remember that things will be phrased in a different way from in the texts themselves.
- Remember that at least one of the texts might not be the answer to any of the statements/questions.

1 You are going to read four reviews of the film *Windtalkers*. For questions 1–4, choose from the reviews A–D. Each review can be chosen more than once.

Review A

Maybe the director, John Woo, did some other kind of work before he discovered that directing films required little or no talent or expertise, but whatever that work was, it didn't do anything to educate him into how things happen in a war. Most of it is unrealistic fantasy. For example, Nicolas Cage, who plays the main character, uses a different kind of gun every time he's on the screen, and this includes one with which he successfully kills several enemy soldiers at a distance of a hundred metres, but which the director should know is not accurate beyond about five metres. It's also incredible that the constant noise of war (explosions, gunfire, screams) ceases the moment Cage needs to talk to one of his buddies. Anyone who hasn't seen it yet should count themselves lucky.

Review B

This film has to be, by far, one of the most inaccurate war films that have ever been. Nicolas Cage is sometimes excellent in films but this is a big miss for him, in my opinion. However, he's far less culpable than the director and the screenwriters, all of whom appear to have done zero research into the war or the Navajo code that the film supposedly is centred around. I say 'supposedly' because if you don't know much about the wonderful story of the code-talkers (as they were called), you will leave this film with no more information than when you went in.

Review C

John Woo is a keen director of war films, having made several before this one. Usually his war films involve a strong mix of action and character portrayal. Here though, the characters definitely take second place. The two principal characters are Joe Enders as a war-weary soldier assigned to protect Ben Yahzee, a Navajo recruit – Yahzee is a code-talker who must not fall into enemy hands and Enders knows that if necessary, he must kill Yahzee to prevent this happening. The two problems here are that there is little evidence that the Navajo code-talkers received such 'protection', and also this is simply not enough to construct a drama that will make us care about either person. The principal actors come out of this well, as do the screenwriters, but over-the-top direction cancels out their efforts.

Review D

The topic of this film centres on how some Native Americans get recruited to work as radio operators using a code based on Navajo that they have developed, and then the efforts of some other soldiers to protect them and the code at all costs. Cage plays one such soldier, and he has Ben Yahzee (Adam Beach) under his wing. One would have hoped that this situation would generate some strong reflections about different people's belief systems, and the director John Woo just about manages to give us an idea of the courage and mental strength required by participants in a war. But the screenwriting just doesn't do enough, and the dialogue between the two central characters did not convince this viewer.

Which reviewer:

1 feels that the director has done better work in the past than on this film? ☐
2 does not mention any concerns about authenticity in the film? ☐
3 suggests that the faults of the film are due entirely to the director? ☐
4 feels the film does not sufficiently educate viewers about the contribution of the Navajos? ☐

CONSOLIDATION

LISTENING

1 🔊 26 Listen to the conversation between Gina and Steve. What is Steve wearing under his suit jacket?

2 🔊 26 Listen again and answer the questions.

1 What is Steve wearing on his feet?

_____

2 Why does Gina object to them?

_____

3 What does Gina recommend he wears?

_____

4 Why will it be hard to find photos of Gina wearing bad fashion?

_____

5 What did Gina use to do with loom bands?

_____

6 What other item did Gina use to wear that she now regrets?

_____

7 What's her biggest piece of fashion advice?

_____

GRAMMAR

3 Match the sentences.

1 Another piece of cake? ☐

2 Do you think we can win? ☐

3 I don't think we've got enough time to walk to the station. ☐

4 Whatever you do, don't tell Ian. ☐

5 Got any chocolate? ☐

6 You used to do yoga. ☐

7 However hard I try I just can't do it. ☐

8 Lucy's got over 500 friends on Facebook. ☐

a Certainly hope so.

b Yes, most of whom she wouldn't recognise if she met them in the street.

c Why not? Is it a secret?

d Still do.

e Love one.

f Don't give up now.

g In which case let's get a taxi.

h Yes, want some?

4 Complete the sentences with the phrases in the list.

both of whom | neither of them | whenever
however | none of which | whoever

1 _____ wrote these homework questions is very cruel.

2 There are 12 questions, _____ I have the slightest idea about.

3 _____ hard I try, I just can't make any sense of them.

4 My mind just goes blank _____ I look at them.

5 I've asked my brothers, _____ think they're good at maths, for help.

6 _____ could help me.

VOCABULARY

5 Complete with the missing words.

1 His interest in cars was very s_____-l_____ and quickly replaced by football.

2 When I hear my five-year-old singing in the school play it brings a t_____ to my e_____.

3 She's quite s_____-c_____ and awkward around people she doesn't know very well.

4 From her b_____ l_____ I would say she's not very impressed by you at all.

5 He speaks French well but his s_____ English a_____ can make him difficult to understand.

6 His speech was incredibly moving. It sent s_____ down my s_____.

7 This new smart phone really is a m_____-h_____ and everyone will be wanting one soon.

8 She's very s_____-a_____ and confident in all she does.

6 Choose the correct option.

1 She's a brilliant pianist but you'd never know because she's so *modest / conceited / expressive*.

2 We are cousins but there's a bit of a language *wall / barrier / fence* between us. Juan's English isn't perfect and my Spanish is virtually non-existent.

3 Jeans never really go *off / out of / in to* fashion.

4 It's so cold he's got *duck / goose / swan* bumps all down his arms.

5 The holiday was great and I just about got by with my *broken / wrecked / damaged* French.

6 She just goes with however she's feeling in the moment. She's very *assertive / forceful / impulsive*.

7 I love a beautiful sunset. It fills my *head / heart / lungs* with joy.

8 Beards are really *all / in / it* at the moment. It seems that all men have got one these days.

DIALOGUE

7 **Put the dialogue in order.**

7	SALESMAN	Exactly, and with Cactus 500X you won't need to spend so much time.
☐	SALESMAN	OK, I'll be quick. Imagine not having to spend half an hour each morning washing your hair.
☐	SALESMAN	OK, let's try something different. With its revolutionary new formula Cactus 500X blends essential hydrating molecules with combing agents and nutritious …
☐	SALESMAN	OK. Just try new Cactus 500X. It's really good for your hair.
1	SALESMAN	Excuse me, Madam. Can I introduce you to our latest shampoo?
☐	SALESMAN	I said, can I introduce you to our latest shampoo, Cactus 500X?
☐	WOMAN	I don't really follow you. I just said that the time I spend washing my hair isn't really a problem for me.
☐	WOMAN	I'm afraid you've lost me. Can you explain it more simply?
☐	WOMAN	OK but be quick, I'm a bit short of time.
☐	WOMAN	I never spend that much time on my hair.
2	WOMAN	Sorry, I didn't catch what you said with all the noise.

READING

8 **Read the article. Complete facts 1–9 with the words in the list. Can you think of the answers to the final act?**

rhythm | feedback | ough | bookkeeper | euouae | pangram | unprosperousness | purple | uncopyrightable

---

AMAZE YOUR FRIENDS WITH …
10 INCREDIBLE FACTS ABOUT THE ENGLISH LANGUAGE.

1 _____ means the state of not being wealthy or profitable. It's not the easiest word to use or remember but is the longest word in English in which each letter is used at least two times.

2 _____ is that horrible noise you get when your microphone is too close to the speaker. It is also the shortest word in English that contains the first six letters of the alphabet.

There are no words in English that rhyme with 'month,' 'orange,' 'silver,' or 3 _____ so don't try using them in a poem (that is if you want it to rhyme).

A 4 _____ is someone who counts the money and does the accounts. It is also the only English word that has three consecutive double letters.

5 _____ is used to describe something such as a photo or a piece of writing that no one has permission to use. More memorably, perhaps, it is the longest English word that contains no letter more than once.

Vowels (a, e, i, o and u) might be the most useful letters in the language. After all, it's pretty difficult to write anything without using one. There is one word, however, you can make: 6 _____.

And at the other extreme, 7 _____ is the longest word in English that contains only vowels. It's a medieval music term but don't ask us exactly what it means or how to pronounce it. Admittedly it's not the most useful word.

The letter combination 8 _____ has nine different ways that it can be pronounced. You'll find them all in the following sentence: 'A rough-coated, dough-faced, thoughtful ploughman strode through the streets of Scarborough; after falling into a slough, he coughed and hiccoughed.' Good luck saying that!

A 9 _____ is a sentence that contains all 26 letters of the alphabet. The most famous example of this is:

'The quick brown fox jumps over the lazy dog.'

And finally, only two English words end in '-gry'. Can you think what they are?

WRITING

9 **Research and write down five amazing facts about your first language.**

GRAMMAR

Negative inversion [SB page 86]

1 ★☆☆ **Circle the correct options.**

Timeless Memories

1 *Never / Little* had Marianne been happier than she was on her wedding day.

2 *Little / Rarely* has a romance been more intense.

3 *Not only / On no account* was Dominic a famous photographer, but he was her dream partner as well.

4 *No sooner / Not only* had they arrived at their hotel than the sun came up.

5 *Little / Never* had they seen a more beautiful dawn.

6 *No sooner / Not only* was the sky wonderful, but the lake sparkled beautifully, too.

7 *Rarely / On no account* do we have the opportunity to photograph something as lovely as that.

8 *Rarely / Under no circumstances* would Marianne let Dominic sell the photos of their trip.

9 *On no account / Not only* could anyone see or publish these photos.

10 *Little / Never* did she know how valuable they would become.

2 ★★☆ **Complete the sentences with a correct form of the verbs in brackets.**

1 Never _____ they _____ a more exciting match than the one on TV last night. (see)

2 On no account _____ Jack _____ to the top of the tower. He's afraid of heights. (climb)

3 No sooner _____ the clock _____ midnight than the spell was broken and Cinderella had to run out of the ballroom. (strike)

4 Rarely _____ we _____ the chance to hear such beautiful music in a shopping centre! (have)

5 Not only _____ the room in the hotel dirty, but the breakfast was awful, too. (be)

6 Never again _____ the river _____ over, because the world is getting warmer. (freeze)

7 Under no circumstances _____ the shop _____ the money because Jane has worn the skirt. (return)

8 Only once every few years _____ Mario _____ his grandparents in South America. (visit)

3 ★★☆ **Rewrite the sentences starting with the word in brackets.**

1 I have never been so shocked by a programme shown on TV. (Never)

_____

2 It was untrue, and wildly exaggerated too. (Not only … but)

_____

3 I don't usually complain about TV programmes. (Rarely)

_____

4 I phoned the TV company immediately after the programme finished. (No sooner … than)

_____

5 The person I spoke to was rude and he seemed to think my complaint was funny. (Not only … but)

_____

6 I had no idea the programme was meant to be a comedy. (Little)

_____

4 ★★★ **There are six sentences in this paragraph which can be changed into negative inversions. Find them and rewrite them using *under no circumstances*, *never*, *not only… but*, *little* and *rarely*.**

Jeb had his dream job working in the garage of a racing team. He worked on the cars and was also allowed to drive them on the test track. The track was designed to test racing cars but the boss told Jeb that he could never go faster than 100 kph. But Jeb was happy just to be in the cars. He had never enjoyed a job so much. Last Tuesday he was taking a car round the track for a final test. Just as he turned the last bend the car slid off the track and crashed into the wall. The boss was furious. 'I don't often see such bad driving from my staff!' he yelled, 'I'll never let you drive again.' But he didn't know that there was oil on the track. When he found out, he apologised to Jeb and said he understood it wasn't his fault and said that of course Jeb could continue to drive the cars.

Spoken discourse markers   SB page 89

5 ★   Circle the correct options.

One person's thoughts about hunting wild animals

1   *To be honest / Let's face it*, I've never been on a hunting trip and I don't want to go.

2   *Personally / If you ask me*, we've done enough harm to wild animals without hunting them.

3   *On the other hand / By the way*, there might be good reasons for reducing the number of animals in over-populated areas.

4   *Personally / Mind you*, it'd be a huge responsibility to have to decide which animals should be killed.

5   *To tell you the truth / However*, there are more humane ways of doing that than hunting.

6   *Let's face it / Because of*, amateur hunters may not always be very good at shooting.

7   *By the way / The thing is*, it's just a matter of who has the money to pay to hunt, you don't have to prove you can shoot.

8   I'm surprised people haven't found an answer yet. *That said / For a start*, it's not an easy problem to solve.

6 ★★★ Five of the underlined discourse markers in this dialogue are incorrect. Find them and replace them with a marker that fits. There is sometimes more than one possibility.

BILL   Andy, do you think it's OK to do what you like with money?

ANDY   Yeah. ¹I mean, if it's my money, why not?

BILL   ²The thing is, I've been reading this book and it raises some interesting questions.

ANDY   Like what?

BILL   ³Nevertheless, is it OK for someone to jump to the front of the queue just because they paid more?

ANDY   ⁴Personally, I think that's OK at an airport or somewhere. ⁵On the other hand, using your time instead of your money is your choice. ⁶As a result, perhaps it's different in somewhere like a hospital. I don't think people should get special treatment because they can pay more. That's not fair.

BILL   ⁷To be honest, I can't see the difference. You're using money to buy privilege.

ANDY   I suppose so. ⁸While I'd do it if I could.

BILL   ⁹Actually, I don't know what to think.

ANDY   Well, ¹⁰at the end of the day, we have to make choices all the time. Don't worry about it. ¹¹For a start, did you finish that history project?

BILL   Huh? Oh yes, the history project …

7 ★★★ Write a short dialogue for two of these situations. Include the discourse markers in the list and any others that are appropriate.

while | however | that said | to tell you the truth
because of | I mean | to be honest | let's face it

a   Vanessa and Steve are talking about a film they watched last night. Vanessa enjoyed it but Steve didn't.

b   Mike and Jane are discussing the test they've just finished. Mike thinks it was easy, Jane doesn't.

c   Karl and Julie are talking about the new restaurant that has opened in the town.

GET IT RIGHT!
Discourse markers

When using discourse markers, learners often position them incorrectly in the sentence.

✓ *Personally*, I don't believe that he's right.

✗ I don't believe ~~personally~~ that he's right.

Identify and underline the discourse marker in each sentence and then tick the sentences which are correct. Rewrite the incorrect ones.

0   I was convinced that the suspect, <u>to be honest</u>, had committed the crime.   ☐

To be honest, I was convinced that the suspect had committed the crime.

1   Let's face it, drugs testing on animals is unethical.   ☐

2   I do believe Kate was treated unfairly. She should have studied harder, that said.   ☐

3   There seems to be a lot in the news about corrupt politicians at the moment. There are lots of other corrupt people mind you too!   ☐

4   The thing is, a lot of people are prejudiced and it's difficult to overcome this.   ☐

5   It isn't really justifiable to spend so much money on prisons when there are so many other important things at the end of the day.   ☐

VOCABULARY

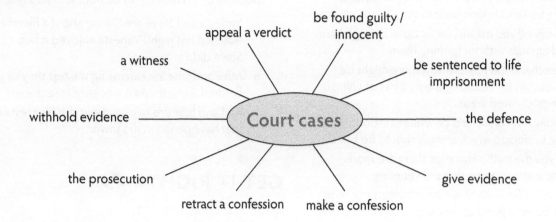

Court cases
- appeal a verdict
- be found guilty / innocent
- a witness
- be sentenced to life imprisonment
- withhold evidence
- the defence
- the prosecution
- give evidence
- retract a confession
- make a confession

Fairness and honesty

acceptable (thing to do)
corrupt
justifiable
prejudiced
reasonable
unbiasedw
unethical

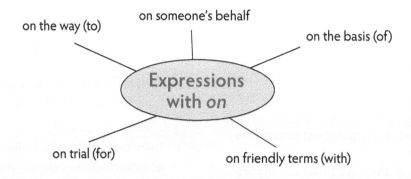

Expressions with *on*
- on the way (to)
- on someone's behalf
- on the basis (of)
- on trial (for)
- on friendly terms (with)

Key words in context

confront	As she left the court, she was **confronted** by a lot of angry people.
convict	The criminal was **convicted** by the court for multiple crimes.
fingerprints	The police have taken the **fingerprints** of every man in the town.
fists	Boxers fight with their **fists**.
innocence	He fought hard to prove his **innocence**, but the court still found him guilty.
interrogation	The police finally let him go home after a two-hour **interrogation**.
intervene	Perhaps the president will **intervene** to help those poor people.
misuse	Some politicians **misuse** their position to make money for themselves.
ordeal	The hostages knew their **ordeal** was over when they saw the police arrive.
solely	We went there **solely** to work – we had no time to enjoy ourselves.
subsequently	He was arrested and **subsequently** put on trial for murder.
throughout	I was bored **throughout** the film – I hated every minute of it.
transplant	The very first heart **transplant** took place in Cape Town in 1967.

Court cases `SB page 86`

1 ★ **Complete the crossword.**

1 A doctor gave … that the accused man was mentally ill.
2 She made a … to the police and said she had committed the crime.
3 The prosecution is not allowed to … evidence from the defence lawyers.
4 The judge said he was … and sent him to prison.
5 There was a … who said he had seen the crime happen.
6 The judge said she was … and she was free to go home.
7 If you think the verdict is wrong, you can …
8 He said that his confession wasn't true and he wanted to … it.
9 In our country, if you murder someone you get sentenced to … imprisonment.
10 There is a lawyer for the prosecution, and one for the …

2 ★★ **Circle the correct options.**

A
I saw the crime and I saw the man who did it. I am certain that Mr Wright is not the man I saw running out of the shop. I believe that Mr Wright is [1]*innocent / guilty*. So I am going to give [2]*evidence / confession* in the court case – I will be a [3]*lawyer / witness* for the [4]*defence / prosecution* and I hope I can help Mr Wright to go home, a free man.

B
When she was arrested, Mrs Ashton made [5]*an appeal / a confession* but later she said that the police had forced her to do so, and that she wanted to [6]*give / retract* what she had said before. She also said, during her trial, that the police had [7]*given / withheld* evidence that would show she was innocent. However, the judge and the jury did not believe her, and they [8]*found / made* her guilty. Mrs Ashton was given a sentence of ten years' [9]*prosecution / imprisonment*.

Fairness and honesty `SB page 89`

3 ★★ **Complete the words in the correct form.**

1 I'm sorry, I just don't think that it's an a_____ thing to do.
2 He was found guilty of c_____ and sent to prison.
3 £25.00 for a ticket? That's fine. I think it's quite r_____, really.
4 Everything she says shows that she has a lot of p_____ against foreigners.
5 It's important that a judge has a completely u_____ view of a trial.
6 I think what they did was u_____ – I mean, you can't just fire someone for being late!
7 There is absolutely no j_____ excuse for that kind of behaviour.

WordWise `SB page 91`
Expressions with *on*

4 ★★ **Match the replies to the mini-dialogues. Then complete the replies with the words in the list.**

behalf | basis | terms | trial | way

1 A Why don't you like me asking you questions?
  B ☐
2 A How's she getting on with the piano?
  B ☐
3 A The police have arrested Mike!
  B ☐
4 A I hear Alice can't come to the meeting.
  B ☐
5 A So, your mother knows the head of the school?
  B ☐

a Because I feel like I'm on _____ for something!
b Yes, they're on pretty friendly _____ with each other.
c That's right, so she's asked me to talk on her _____ .
d Really well! She's on her _____ to being a very good player.
e I know, but I don't understand on what _____ he's being accused.

READING

1 REMEMBER AND CHECK Match the names with the phrases. Then read the article on page 85 in the Student's Book again and check.

1 Sally Clark

2 Rubin Carter

3 Gerry Conlon (of the Guildford Four)

a spent eighteen years in jail.

b was a lawyer.

c was accused of killing soldiers and their girlfriends.

d spent three years in jail.

e was played by Daniel Day-Lewis in a film.

f had a song written about him.

g had an alibi for when the crime was committed.

h retracted an initial confession.

2 Read the blog and choose the best title for it.

A Are you as fair as you think you are?

B Why fairness matters to people

C How different people define 'fairness'

3 Read the blog again and answer the questions.

1 What two things need to be balanced for something to be fair?

_____

2 What are many people not willing to do?

_____

3 What did the writer try to do when compiling the quiz?

_____

4 Which of the situations concerns damage to property?

_____

5 Which situation has nothing to do with money?

_____

6 What was the writer's real purpose in compiling the quiz?

_____

4 Think of another situation for the quiz. Write it and end with the question 'Is this fair?' Then write your answer and give your reasons.

One thing that seems to be a feature of all human beings is a notion of fairness – but what does it really mean? Most people would agree that it means thinking about the needs and interests of other people when making decisions about how to behave, and striking a balance between our needs and theirs. OK, but does everybody share the same idea of what's fair and what isn't? Clearly not! There's a lot of variation between individual people and between cultures – some people tend to be more selfish, inconsiderate and colder than others. Yet if you ask people 'Are you a fair person?' almost everyone will answer 'Yes,' won't they? Let's face it, not many people are willing to put up their hands and say 'I don't think I'm a fair person,' or, 'the world isn't fair, so neither am I'!

So, what about you – are you a fair person? I've put together a 'quiz' – some questions for you to answer either 'Yes' or 'No' to see how fair you really are. How would you answer these questions?

1 A mother and father have two children – one aged 15, one aged 9. They give the same monthly pocket money to each child. Is this fair?

2 Someone lends you a book, and accidentally you tear the corner of one of the pages. You tell this to the person who lent you the book – the person asks you to buy them a new book. Is this fair?

3 You are standing in a queue to get some coffee in a coffee shop. Someone runs past everyone in the queue, saying 'Sorry, I'm really late!' and goes to the front of the queue. Is this fair?

4 A student has to write an essay for school. Another student offers to write the paper for them, for £50. The first student accepts, pays and gets top marks. Is this fair?

5 The electricity workers are on strike and homes have no electricity, so people have to use battery-powered torches. Some shopkeepers increase the price of their torches and batteries. Is this fair?

6 There is a school in a town that has the best facilities and the best teachers, but they only accept students whose parents have enough money to pay the school fees. Is this fair?

Of course, this quiz can't possibly tell us if you treat people fairly or not in real life, can it? So, what's the point? Well, it shows us that in every one of the six situations there are two sides to every story, and that we should always try to see the other person's point of view, even if we think there is only one correct answer.

Pronunciation

Unstressed syllables and words: the /ɪ/ phoneme

Go to page 120.

DEVELOPING WRITING

An essay

1 Read the essay and choose the correct options.

1 The essay is mainly about …
   A the need to make punishments for certain crimes more severe.
   B not punishing unemployed people.
   C adjusting punishments according to who committed the crime.

2 The writer believes that judges …
   A are too strict when they sentence people.
   B should choose from a range of punishments.
   C should punish 40-year-old people more strictly than 17-year-old people.

The punishment should fit the crime – and the criminal.

Some people believe that for each type of criminal <u>offence</u>, the person responsible should receive the same punishment, no matter what the circumstances. ¹_____, I believe that the system which we have in place now in the UK, whereby judges can <u>use their discretion</u> when sentencing someone, is far better.

Let us take an example. ²_____ that the fixed sentence for shoplifting is a three-month jail sentence. This means that every person caught shoplifting would go to prison for three months, no matter who the person is (or what they stole). ³_____, it is not at all difficult to see that such a situation would be unfair. Once we begin to consider differences between people, like their age or their personal circumstances, it becomes clear that a judge needs to be able to choose from within a range of possible sentences.

Should a 17-year-old unemployed person, convicted of shoplifting for the first time, be given the same sentence as a 40-year-old employed person who has been <u>convicted</u> several times before? I do not believe so. ⁴_____, I would argue that it would be completely wrong to give the 17-year-old <u>first-time offender</u> a prison sentence: that would be far too <u>severe</u> and it would also put them into contact with other criminals. Something more <u>lenient</u> would be more appropriate – for example, <u>community service</u> and a suspended sentence.
⁵_____, someone who has offended many times should go to prison for more than just three months.

⁶_____, it is my opinion that judges should have a range of sentencing options available to them for most offences, which allows them <u>to take into account</u> the circumstances both of the crime and of the person involved.

2 Complete the essay with the words in the list.

Arguably | Consequently | However
Imagine | In fact | Now

3 Find an underlined word or phrase which means …

1 an action which is against the law
   _____

2 someone who had not committed a crime before _____

3 found guilty in a court of law _____

4 work that is to help other people, and is done without payment (sometimes as a punishment) _____

5 not kind or showing sympathy _____

6 to consider or remember something when judging a situation _____

7 use their right or ability to decide something
   _____

8 not strong in punishment _____

4 You are going to write an essay titled 'Shaming offenders'. Make notes on the positive and negative points of this idea.

Sometimes a judge might decide to 'shame' someone as punishment for a crime they've committed. For example, a shoplifter might be sent back to the shop to stand outside with a sign that says 'I stole from this shop.'

5 Write your essay. Write 250–300 words.

- do some internet research for examples of 'shaming'
- state what shaming consists of
- say what your overall opinion is
- give examples of how this is a positive or negative idea

CHECKLIST ✓

LISTENING

1 🔊 **28 Listen to two boys talking about a film. Tick the statement below which is NOT true.**

- [ ] **a** It's about a doctor who is accused of murder.
- [ ] **b** The doctor escapes and runs away.
- [ ] **c** A detective catches the doctor again.

2 🔊 **28 Listen again. Complete each statement with one or two words.**

1 Kimble is a happily married _____ .
2 He fights a _____ man who has killed his wife.
3 He is sentenced _____ for the murder.
4 He escapes from a train when _____ a bus.
5 He goes back to Chicago to _____ the real killer.
6 He escapes another time by _____ a big waterfall, and he survives.
7 The detective says he _____ whether Kimble is guilty or not.
8 The boy telling the story _____ who the killer is.

DIALOGUE

1 Put the dialogues in order.

Dialogue 1

- [ ] **MO** No, it doesn't. And more to the point, that's six years of his life that he'll never get back. He's in his mid-50s now.
- [1] **MO** Did you hear about that man who got released from prison?
- [ ] **MO** I'm not sure, but I'd have thought it won't be easy for him to restart his life.
- [ ] **MO** Or even longer. It can be hard for people who've left prison to find a job.
- [ ] **MO** Something like six years, if I'm not mistaken. And for something he didn't do!
- [ ] **SAM** Wow, that's a long time. It really doesn't seem fair, does it?
- [ ] **SAM** Well, I heard something, yes. How long had he been in prison?
- [ ] **SAM** You're right, it'll take some time – around a couple of months, I'd think.
- [ ] **SAM** Well, when you put it like that, it sounds even worse. Poor guy. What do you think he'll do now?

Dialogue 2

- [ ] **ALICE** Really? So, how much is too much?
- [ ] **ALICE** OK, sorry. Well, it's a shame you can't come. Maybe next month?
- [1] **ALICE** Do you want to come out tonight? I'm meeting up with Jack and the others.
- [ ] **ALICE** That doesn't seem fair. Why on earth have they done that?
- [ ] **ALICE** Well when you put it like that, I can see what your parents mean.
- [ ] **LUCY** Hey, you're supposed to be my best friend – don't take my parents' side!
- [ ] **LUCY** Well I'd like to but I can't. My parents have told me I can only go out twice a month.
- [ ] **LUCY** Well, one evening last month I spent in the region of £30, give or take. It was just under my whole allowance for the month.
- [ ] **LUCY** Oh, they say I've got to do more studying. And more to the point, they reckon I spend too much.

PHRASES FOR FLUENCY SB page 91

1 Complete the phrases with the missing words.

0 *apparently*
1 I'd _____ thought
2 more _____ _____ point
3 it's _____ _____ me
4 if _____ not _____
5 _____ you _____ it _____ that

2 Use a word or phrase from Exercise 1 to complete the mini-dialogues.

1 **A** This is a cool song. Who's the singer?
 B Good question. Um, it's Adele, _____ .

2 **A** Did you know she's a really good chess player?
 B No, _____ .

3 **A** What happened to Mike? I heard he's in hospital.
 B That's right. _____ he fell over and broke his arm.

4 **A** I don't like the colour of that shirt.
 B Oh? That's strange. _____ it would be something you'd like.

5 **A** I think it was the worst film I've ever seen.
 B Really? Well, _____ , maybe I won't go and see it.

6 **A** Why didn't you buy it?
 B It was a bit expensive and _____ , I wasn't 100% sure I liked it.

Listening part 2

1 ◀ⅉ29 You will hear a woman called Monica talking about a month of work experience she did at a supermarket. For questions 1–8, complete the sentences with a word or short phrase.

MONICA'S WORK EXPERIENCE

Monica's work experience at the supermarket involved (1) _____ managers at various levels.

Monica states that the experience was (2) _____ as to how supermarkets really operate.

Monica says she (3) _____ about what she thought the nature of supermarkets was.

Someone had to be present at the supermarket at five in the morning when the (4) _____ started to arrive.

Monica uses the words (5) '_____' to describe the fact that she had to go in at 5 am several times a week.

For Monica, being allowed to go home at 2 pm (6) _____ for the early starts.

Monica felt that the manager of the supermarket looked at the employees as if they were (7) _____.

The manager and the other employees had (8) _____ for each other.

Writing part 2

2 Write an answer to the question. Write your answer in 220–260 words in an appropriate style.

A report

You went to an English-speaking country and spent a month doing work experience.

The person who organised the work experience for you would like you to write a report explaining what the work was like and how you felt about the experience.

Write your report. (You can choose the kind of work experience you did – e.g. a factory, an office, a bank, a school, etc.)

GRAMMAR
Reported verb patterns (review) SB page 94

1 ★☆☆ **Complete the phrases with the correct preposition.**

1 apologise _____ doing something
2 promise _____ do something
3 blame someone _____ doing something
4 decide _____ do something
5 insist _____ doing something
6 convince (someone) not _____ do something

2 ★★☆ **Complete the sentences with the correct form of the verb in brackets.**

1 I recommend _____ (study) civil engineering at university.
2 My dad suggested _____ (take) a gap year.
3 My sister regrets _____ (not go) to university.
4 My brother has decided _____ (apply) to do a degree at Bath University.
5 I blamed myself for _____ (not pass) my English Literature A-Level.
6 York University has invited me _____ (speak) at a conference in March.

3 ★★☆ **Rewrite the sentences using reported verb patterns.**

0 'You passed! Well done,' Sam congratulated me.
   Sam congratulated me on passing.
1 'You need to work harder,' warned Ms Gibbs.
   _____
2 'You must go straight to university,' my parents insisted.
   _____
3 'I've made a mistake,' admitted Jasper.
   _____
4 'You could apply for a job instead of applying for university,' my head teacher suggested.
   _____

4 ★★☆ **Complete the news story with the correct verb patterns using the verb in brackets.**

In 2015, a British exam board promised [1]_____ (change) their A-level music syllabus after a London teenager, Jesse McCabe, won her campaign to ensure female composers were studied on the course. The exam board apologised [2]_____ (not feature) a single woman amongst the 63 composers. The board decided [3]_____ (ask) leading academics who they felt should be included. Several of them suggested [4]_____ (include) the 19th century German musician Clara Schumann and 17th century Italian Baroque singer Barbara Strozzi. The board also agreed [5]_____ (review) their other qualifications to ensure they were diverse and inclusive. The Managing Director personally apologised to the 17-year-old student [6]_____ (not include) women on their A-Level syllabus. Other examining boards were also warned [7]_____ (review) their syllabuses. Many academics regretted [8]_____ (not make) changes to their syllabuses earlier.

5 ★★★ **Use the prompts to complete the dialogue. Use the correct verb patterns.**

A I heard that your bike got stolen. Then you saw it up for sale on an online website. What did you do?
B [1]My friends / recommend / tell / the police
   _____
A That sounds sensible to me. Then what did you do?
B [2]The police / warn / me / not / contact / the thief
   _____
   Then the police went to the thief's house.
A And what happened when they got to the house?
B [3]The police / accuse / man / steal / bike
   _____
   [4]He / confess / steal / it
   _____
   [5]He / apologise / take / it
   _____
   [6]And / he / promise / never / steal / anything / again
   _____

Passive report structures `SB page 97`

6 ★★ **Complete the theories about the benefits of studying certain subjects with a passive report structure. Use the verbs in brackets.**

1 Subjects such as Art, Music and Foreign Languages _____ have long-lasting benefits. (say)

2 Visual thinking _____ help children learn other subjects. (know)

3 Children who learn a musical instrument as a child _____ be able to listen and communicate better as adults. (believe)

4 It _____ children and adults who play a musical instrument for 30 minutes a week over the course of a year will have more highly developed brains. (think)

5 Exercise _____ extremely important for the cognitive development of children's brains. (consider)

7 ★★ **Rewrite the sentences using passive report structures.**

1 New research has found that 59% of UK graduates would choose a positive workplace over a better salary. (find)

It _____

2 In the UK in 2015, 60% of 2013/2014 graduates were working in a job that didn't require a degree. (report)

It _____

3 Research has established that in 2015, only 55% of 2013/2014 graduates were working in their chosen field. (establish)

It _____

4 A recruitment agency warned companies that if they failed to create career development programmes, they would miss the opportunity of attracting top talent. (warn)

Companies _____

5 By 2015, only 58% of 2013/2014 graduates had found secure full-time work. (confirm)

It _____

Hedging `SB page 97`

8 ★★ **Rewrite the sentences with the 'vague' language in the list. Use each expression only once.**

~~might~~ | thought that | It is believed that | said to
seems to | probably won't

0 Fruit lowers the risk of cancer.

Fruit *might lower the risk of cancer.*

1 It has been proved that eating pomegranates can strengthen your bones.

It is _____ .

2 Eating garlic will prevent you from catching a cold.

You _____ if you eat garlic.

3 Your memory will improve if you include blueberries in your diet.

Adding blueberries to your diet is

_____ .

4 Drinking green tea will help you lose weight.

Drinking green tea _____ .

5 Eating oily fish two or three times a week will protect your eyesight in old age.

_____ .

GET IT RIGHT! 👁
Passive report structures

Learners often make mistakes when using passive report structures.

✓ *Beethoven is believed **to have composed** his first piece of music when he was three.*

✗ *Beethoven is believed ~~to compose~~ his first piece of music when he was three.*

Rewrite the sentences making the underlined words the subject of each sentence.

1 It is reported that the government has plans to make cuts to the education budget.

_____

2 It was thought at one time that the world was flat.

_____

3 It is known that having a gap year can be beneficial to character development.

_____

4 It was found that the dissertation had been plagiarised.

_____

5 It is said that the family next door won the lottery last year.

_____

6 It is reported that the US president is going to visit the UK.

VOCABULARY

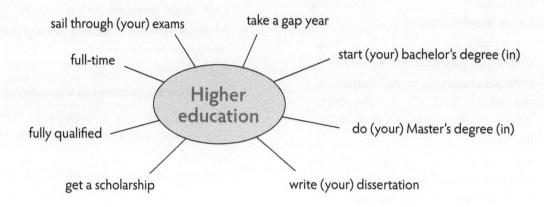

Life after school

do	take	go	get
voluntary work an apprenticeship military service	a gap year	to university	a full-time job

Key words in context

boast	The boy **boasted** that he was the best athlete in the school.
empathise	We all felt sorry for him when he failed the Physics exam. We all knew what it was like to fail an exam and we **empathised** with him.
enhance (your) prospects	If you try and improve your marks, it will **enhance your prospects** of being offered a place at your chosen university.
exposed to	Sibel was **exposed to** classical music for the first time when she went to the Philharmonic Orchestra concert last night.
innovation	Technology is always changing and improving and every year there are new **innovations**.
mumbled	Her **mumbled** reply to my question was difficult for me to hear.
raise (your) voice	Our Maths teacher never gets angry and never **raises her voice** in class. She always remains calm.
refute	The head teacher **refuted** the claim that too many students were failing their exams. He said that students were getting good marks now.
striking	I remember the man because he was wearing a **striking** blue jacket. He really stood out in the crowd.
valid	Your railcard is no longer **valid**. Look! It lasts for a year and you bought it two years ago.

Higher education SB page 94

1 ★★ **Unscramble the words in brackets to complete the dialogue.**

ELLA   Well, you finally finished writing that [1]_____ (sserditatnio), and you [2]_____ (adslie) through your final exams. Well done! So now you've got your [3]_____ (chabelro's) degree, what are you going to do?

FINN   I'm hoping to do a [4]_____ (saMret's) degree next. I've been offered a place at Bristol University, but I can't afford to go unless I get a [5]_____ (loschrapish).

ELLA   Good luck. I'm sure you'll get it.

FINN   Thanks. What about you? What are you going to do?

ELLA   I'm a [6]_____ (ylluf fiedilaqu) engineer now. So if all goes well I'll be in [7]_____ (lufl-mite) work by this time next year. But in the meantime, I'm going to enjoy taking a [8]_____ (apg ryea).

2 ★★ **Match the words/phrases in Exercise 1 to the definitions.**

☐ a   an advanced college or university degree

☐ b   to succeed very easily in something, especially a test

☐ c   a long piece of writing on a particular subject, especially one that is done in order to receive a degree at college or university

☐ d   done for the whole of a working week

☐ e   having finished a training course, or having particular skills, etc.

☐ f   a first degree at college or university

☐ g   a year between leaving school and starting university that is usually spent travelling or working

☐ h   an amount of money given by a university to pay for studies of a person with great ability but little money

Life after school SB page 95

3 ★★ **Circle the correct verbs to complete the questions. Then write true answers for you.**

1   A   Do you have to *get* / *do* military service in your country?
    YOU _____

2   A   Do you know anyone who *took* / *did* a gap year before starting university?
    YOU _____

3   A   Do you know anyone didn't *go to* / *have* university straight after school?
    YOU _____

4   A   Do you think it's possible to *go* / *get* a full-time job whilst you're at university?
    YOU _____

5   A   Do you think it's a good idea to *do* / *get* some voluntary work in the holidays?
    YOU _____

6   A   Do you know anyone who has *done* / *gone* an apprenticeship?
    YOU _____

4 ★★ **Complete the sentences with a verb in the correct tense.**

Orhan [1]_____ to Warwick University to study Art History. He [2]_____ (not) a gap year before university. In his third year, he [3]_____ voluntary work at an art gallery in Mexico City. After finishing university, he returned home to Turkey and he [4]_____ his military service. Now he wants [5]_____ a full-time job. His brother [6]_____ (not) to university. He [7]_____ an apprenticeship instead. Now, he has a good job and he earns a lot of money.

5 ★★★ **Write sentences that are true for you. Use the words in brackets.**

After leaving school, …

1   (apprenticeship) _____
2   (university) _____
3   (full-time job) _____
4   (gap year) _____
5   (military service) _____
6   (voluntary work) _____

Pronunciation

Lexical and non-lexical fillers

Go to page 121.

READING

1 REMEMBER AND CHECK **Answer the questions. Then read the review on page 93 of the Student's Book again and check.**

1 What question from the audience started a good debate on *Face the Questions*?

_____

2 Which school subjects did the politicians say they would never cut?

_____

3 What does JoJo71 suggest is a good way of learning kindness and respect?

_____

4 Why does Ballboy12 think it's important to teach Economics at school?

_____

5 What does Olliepops say Geography can give you?

_____

6 Which problem does Ajay22 say sport and exercise help to fight?

_____

2 **Read the article quickly. What is the aim of the research project, Teensleep?**

_____

3 **Read the article again and mark the sentences T (true) or F (false).**

1 Scientists believe that early school start times are not in the best interests of any children. ☐

2 Previous research had been done on the influence of school start times on children but nothing as extensive as this one. ☐

3 After the age of 24, we start shifting our biological clocks back to earlier in the 24-hour cycle. ☐

4 People in their late teens are typically getting around two hours' sleep less than they need on a nightly basis. ☐

5 Convention has dictated traditional school start times. ☐

6 Dr Kelley is convinced that sleep deprivation explains the high incidence of mental illness in those in their late teens. ☐

4 **Do you think starting school at a later time will help your concentration and improve your performance at school? Write a short paragraph listing the advantages and disadvantages.**

Teensleep

Schools across Britain are being asked to take part in a research project to stagger their start times to suit the different biological clocks of children, with ten-year-olds starting at 9 am and 15-year-olds starting at 10 am. Scientists believe that the body's circadian rhythm, which determines sleep-wake patterns over 24-hour periods, varies with a child's age and that an earlier school start time for all students is not in the best interests of older children. The research project, funded by the Wellcome Trust, will recruit 100 schools as part of the biggest study yet into the role that school start times play in the education and wellbeing of students, said Paul Kelley of the University of Oxford.

The natural shift in the biological clock to later in the 24-hour cycle is particularly acute in the 14 to 24 age group. The shift in the biological clock continues in later middle age, when people usually revert to the naturally earlier start time they felt comfortable with when they were 10-year-old children, Dr Kelley said.

'We cannot change our 24-hour rhythms. You cannot learn to get up at a particular time. By the time you are 18, 19 or 20 you are getting up and going to sleep up to two or three hours earlier on average, depending on the time of year,' Dr Kelley said. 'You are suffering on average two hours of sleep loss a day and that is cumulative so that at the end of the week you have suffered 10 hours of sleep loss. It has a hugely damaging impact on the body,' he told the Science Festival in Bradford.

'Students lose more sleep than doctors working a 24-hour shift during every school or university week … Schools are arbitrarily starting at any time they choose. There is no justification and no study suggesting that starting earlier is better,' he said. 'Most people wake up to alarms because they don't naturally wake up at the time they go to work, so we are a sleep-deprived society and this age group, 14 to 24, is more deprived than any other sector of society,' he added.

The research project, known as Teensleep, will investigate whether there are any benefits in starting school later for the GCSE age group of 14–16 years. Other studies in the US have suggested that students in colleges and universities aged 18 and older can benefit from an even later start time of 11 am, he said.

[…] 'The kinds of changes at this age are quite dramatic – 50% of mental illnesses occur at this age … It may be that part of the problem is a circadian time shift and a sleep-deprivation problem,' Dr Kelley said. 'It is a bit of an ask to go to your school governing body to say that we need to change our times but the mood in the place changes for the better – there are more emotional interactions,' he said. 'This applies to the bigger picture, to employers, to prisons, to hospitals where everyone is woken up at 6 am to be given food they do not want,' he told the meeting.

DEVELOPING WRITING

An essay

1 Read the writing task, then number the paragraphs of the essay in the correct order.

> **Read the quote and then write an essay to answer the question.**
>
> 'British industry needs 40,000 more scientists, engineers and technicians each year, forcing many companies to seek out highly-trained foreigners to fill the vacancies in the workforce.'

How can more young people be encouraged to take engineering courses at university?

☐ To address the first and second issues, I would encourage students with an interest in arts subjects to see the creative side to engineering. Show them that it isn't all just about maths. Let students see the links between design and engineering, and also show how it is linked to other industries that young people might be interested in such as the catering industry and hospitals. You could also show them that there are options to travel and work abroad.

☐ Primary schools and secondary schools need to be given more information about what exactly engineering is and how interesting and rewarding it could be as a career. Companies could set engineering challenges for school students. Tours of work places, talks and practical projects could be given by companies. Another possibility would be to give students a financial incentive to study engineering. Lower the course fees and offer more scholarships.

☐ In conclusion, I believe that firstly, engineering companies need to have more links with schools to show children exactly what engineering entails and to show them it can be just as exciting and creative a career as journalism or architecture. Secondly, the government needs to create financial incentives to study engineering as it is important for this country's future.

☐ In my opinion, there are three main reasons why students are put off studying engineering, and these issues need to be addressed. Firstly, students think that you need to be good at maths to study engineering. Secondly, it is not seen as a creative or glamorous career choice. Thirdly, and perhaps most importantly, students often don't know much about engineering.

2 The sample essay has looked at engineering. Now write an essay discussing how you would encourage school students to choose one of the careers below. Write 220–280 words.

medicine | law | art history | business and management | architecture | transportation planning
marine biology | archaeology | film & theatre | translation | teaching

You may use some of the ideas expressed in the sample essay, but you should use your own ideas as far as possible. Think about how to motivate students and what incentives you could give.

Writing tip: an essay

Before writing, make a list of all the possible ways to encourage students.

For example, architecture:

- Take students on visits to see buildings of interest in your town.
- Look at your school. Is it well designed? Which features and facilities work well?
- What could be improved?
- Organise a design competition: Design a building.
- Study materials used in building.

LISTENING

1 🔊31 **Listen to the conversation between three friends and note down four reasons given for banning mobile phones.**

1 _____

2 _____

3 _____

4 _____

2 🔊31 **Listen to the dialogue again and mark the sentences T (true), F (false) or DS (doesn't say).**

1 Max is not happy to hear that mobile phones will be banned from school. ☐

2 Emma says it's hard for students to concentrate in class when they are allowed to use their mobile phones. ☐

3 Emma says students' grades would improve if they didn't use mobile phones in school. ☐

4 Most mobile phones are stolen from students aged between 13 and 16. ☐

5 One in fifteen children aged 8 to 16 will have their mobile phone stolen. ☐

6 There is a danger that a child texting while crossing the road may be involved in an accident. ☐

7 Max thinks banning mobile phones will just cause more problems. ☐

8 The mobile phone ban will be put into practice next year. ☐

DIALOGUE

1 **Complete the dialogues with the phrases in the list.**

I'm glad to hear it | What will they think of next
I think it's about time | They've got to be joking
That's outrageous | That's the best news I've heard in ages

Dialogue 1

MEL Have you heard the fast food restaurant opposite school is being closed down? Apparently the school has complained about it being there. They say it encourages students to make bad food choices.

SUSIE ¹_____? Take away the vending machine, too? I think we should be able to choose what we want to eat.

MEL Personally, ²_____. The food there's horrible – plastic burgers in plastic buns and horrible greasy chips. I don't think there's any real meat in the burgers.

SUSIE How would you know? You're a vegetarian.

Dialogue 2

JOHN ³_____ they did something about the school chemistry lab. All the equipment in there is falling to pieces.

SARAH Haven't you heard? Mr Morris took it up with the school board last week and some money is being allocated to buying new equipment.

JOHN ⁴_____. But how did you find out about it?

SARAH I've been complaining to my mum about it for months. She was at the meeting last week and she told me.

JOHN Why didn't you tell me earlier then?

Dialogue 3

AMY I'm afraid I've got some bad news for you, Joe.

JOE What now?

AMY The school isn't letting anyone take A-Level Art as of next year.

JOE ⁵_____, surely! The only reason I want to stay on at school is to take Art.

AMY I knew you'd be upset.

JOE ⁶_____. They'll be cancelling Music lessons and P.E. soon I expect.

AMY They can't do that.

JOE If they can cancel Art lessons for sixth formers, they can cancel Music. You wait, that will be next on the list.

2 **Now write a new dialogue. Complain to a friend about something that has happened or will happen at school that you disagree with. Include some of the phrases from Exercise 1.**

Listening part 4

Exam guide: multiple matching

In Listening part 4, you will hear five speakers talk about a common topic. For this task, you will need to listen out for the speaker's opinion, attitude or feeling about something. You will need to answer two sets of questions and you will only hear each extract twice.

- Read both sets of questions first.
- Remember, there are three extra options that you won't use in each task.
- Listen for similar themes: Is it about the past or the future? This will help you in choosing the answers.
- While you listen you must complete both tasks.

1   ◀ᴺ32 You will hear five short extracts in which people are talking about different aspects of education.

Task one

For questions 1–5, choose from the list (A–H) each speaker's opinion.

A   University is not for everyone and that's OK.

B   Practical skills are more useful to some people than academic study.

C   Being able to spell is an essential skill.

D   It's impossible to get a good job if you don't have a degree.

E   Too much importance is being placed on teaching literacy in schools.

F   A lot of life skills can be learned from play.

G   Real work experience needs to be part of the course.

H   Students need to spend more time revising for exams.

1   Speaker 1   ☐

2   Speaker 2   ☐

3   Speaker 3   ☐

4   Speaker 4   ☐

5   Speaker 5   ☐

Task two

For questions 6–10, choose from the list (A–H) what advice each speaker gives.

A   If you fail in school you will be a failure all your life.

B   There are other options besides university.

C   You may not do well in school but you will find a job that suits you.

D   Students should be examined less.

E   Students' self-confidence needs to be developed.

F   Try not to misunderstand your emails.

G   Don't take exams too seriously. It doesn't matter if you fail them.

H   Don't neglect your literacy skills.

6   Speaker 1   ☐

7   Speaker 2   ☐

8   Speaker 3   ☐

9   Speaker 4   ☐

10   Speaker 5   ☐

CONSOLIDATION

LISTENING

1 🔊33 Listen to a man complaining about something. What does he think is unfair?

2 🔊33 Listen again and answer the questions.

1 Why were the queues for some rides really long?

_____

2 While he was in the queue, what did the man see that he described as 'odd'?

_____

3 How does the queue jumper work?

_____

4 Why does the man think the queue jumper system is unfair?

_____

5 What do some airports offer that annoys the man?

_____

6 What is the man's overall opinion about money?

_____

GRAMMAR

3 Put the words in order to make sentences.

1 insisted / washing / me / on / doing / Mum / the / up / .

_____

2 of / silly / At / the / day / only / it's / a / the / game / end / .

_____

3 the / for / TV / Dad / me / blamed / breaking / .

_____

4 I / apologise / will / circumstances / to / Under / Maria / no / .

_____

5 been / the / believed / to / He / involved / in / robbery / is / have / .

_____

6 It's / solved / the / never / might / thought / that / mystery / be / .

_____

7 I / in / the / No / shower / had / than / the / sooner / phone / rang / got / .

_____

VOCABULARY

4 Match the sentence halves.

1 My mother had to go to court to give ☐
2 He's smart and we expect he'll sail ☐
3 Because of the seriousness of the crime he was ☐
4 I'm considering taking ☐
5 He felt so guilty he made ☐
6 My parents couldn't afford that school but I got ☐
7 She spends every Saturday doing ☐
8 My brother's writing his ☐

a sentenced to life imprisonment.
b a confession to the police.
c dissertation on Eastern European politics.
d evidence in a trial.
e voluntary work helping with the elderly.
f a gap year before I go to university.
g a scholarship and studied there for free.
h through his end of year exams.

5 Compete the sentences with the words in the list.

reasonable | verdict | corrupt | terms
innocent | unethical | witness | trial

1 The politician was hugely _____ and used his position to make thousands of pounds.

2 She's on _____ for stealing money from her boss.

3 Don't worry. Mr Bowden's a _____ man and he'll understand you had a problem.

4 I know Daniel but we're not exactly on friendly _____ .

5 We're very unhappy with the _____ and we will be appealing against it.

6 Although it wasn't illegal, it was _____ and you shouldn't have done it.

7 He was found _____ and all charges against him were dropped.

8 Although the crime took place in a crowded street, the police could not find a single _____ .

DIALOGUE

6 Complete the dialogue with the phrases in the list. There are two you won't use.

action | region | or less | do that | or take
be joking | something | outrageous

BOB It's going to cost you £30,000 more
¹ _____ if you want to go to
university.

ALICE £30,000? That's ² _____ .

BOB And that's only for tuition. With
accommodation and food you're
looking at ³ _____ like
£50,000.

ALICE That's absurd.

BOB And now universities are increasing
their fees even more.

ALICE That's not fair. They can't
⁴ _____ .

BOB No, they can't, which is why we're
organising a protest next week.

ALICE Finally, someone's taking
⁵ _____ .

BOB Yes, we're expecting something
in the ⁶ _____ of 100,000
students to join.

ALICE Well make that 100,001 because I'm
definitely going.

READING

7 Read the article and complete the table.

	rule	reason
food		
language		
recreation		
clothing		

WRITING

8 Invent a crazy school rule. Write an
announcement explaining the rule and
the reasons for it.

Every school needs a solid set of rules which help guide their students and let them know what will and won't be tolerated. Most school rules are based on a set of sound and sensible principles. However, occasionally there are cases when schools have been known to take things one step too far. Here are some of the more interesting cases to have made it into the papers.

A school in Essex has banned its dinner ladies from serving a type of biscuit known as flapjack in the shape of a triangle. The decision was reached after a student was hit in the face by a piece of triangular flapjack that had been thrown by another pupil. From now on, flapjack must be cut into square or rectangular portions.

Another school in Croydon, London has banned its students from using slang. On the list of forbidden items are words such as 'ain't' (is not), 'innit' (isn't it), 'coz' (because) and 'you/we woz'. The school took the decision in an attempt to make their students more employable. The school believes that students who use such informal language will find it more difficult to get jobs when they leave.

Morning break has long been a time when students can release all the energy they've stored up while sitting in lessons by playing football or some other activity involving running around the playground for half an hour. Not any more for students at a school in Connecticut, US, which has put a ban on such activities as the authorities fear they could provoke physical or emotional damage. Instead students are encouraged to jump ropes or gently throw Frisbees. Supervised games of 'kickball' are occasionally allowed but only if the score is not kept.

Clothing is often an area of controversy and there are many stories of students who have been sent home because their clothes contravene what's acceptable within the school rules. But one of the more unusual items to have been banned are  Ugg-type boots. Winters in Pennsylvania can be extremely cold and these fur-lined boots could be seen as the ideal footwear for keeping students' feet warm and dry. Not so according to one school in the area, which has forbidden students from wearing them to school. The reason? Apparently, they offer the perfect place for smuggling mobile phones into the school!

GRAMMAR

More on the passive `SB page 104`

1 ★☆☆ **Circle the correct verb. Sometimes both options are possible.**

1 We *were / got* soaked walking home in the rain.

2 When she tried to leave, she discovered the door *was / got* locked.

3 Tom told his mother he didn't know how the TV *was / got* broken.

4 Sally ran into the road without looking and *was / got* hit by a car.

5 She *was / got* loved by everyone who knew her.

6 My case *was / got* put on the wrong plane and went to China!

2 ★★☆ **Replace the verb *be* with *get* where possible.**

1 Some strange lights were seen in the sky and there was a lot of talk of UFOs.

2 Gina was stopped for speeding by a police patrol.

3 You might be mugged if you wear a gold watch on that beach.

4 James was heard talking to his girlfriend on the office phone.

5 After his interview on TV, Steve was phoned by a lot of people he didn't know.

6 When my mother tidied my bedroom some of my favourite things were thrown away.

3 ★★★ **Rewrite these sentences, starting with the words given. Use *get* wherever possible.**

1 Somebody stole my suitcase while I was asleep.
My suitcase _____ .

2 Helen's mother told her off for being late home.
Helen _____ .

3 Somebody saw the man leaving the bank with a bag.
The man _____ .

4 Some kids throwing stones hurt my cat.
My cat _____ .

5 My grandmother loved the new baby.
The new baby _____ .

6 People talk about film stars a lot.
Film stars _____ .

Causative *have* (review) `SB page 105`

4 ★★☆ **Complete the gaps with the correct form of *have* and the verbs given.**

0 My hair's too long. I must _____*have*_____ it _____*cut*_____ . (cut)

1 My car needs a paint job. I will _____ it _____ . (repaint)

2 The carpet was very dirty. We _____ it _____ . (clean)

3 Their garden wall was damaged in the accident. They _____ it _____ . (rebuild)

4 The old garage was falling down so we had to _____ it _____ . (demolish)

5 She hated the tattoo, so she _____ it _____ by laser. (remove)

5 ★★☆ **Complete the gaps in the dialogue with the correct form of *have* and words from the list.**

installed | replaced | put in | changed
repaired | painted

JIM   Hi, Harry! I heard your new house was broken into. So awful! Was anything stolen?

HARRY   No, but we had [1]_____ a new back door _____ before we could move in. And, of course, we needed to [2]_____ the locks _____ .

JIM   When did you eventually move in?

HARRY   Last month. We [3]_____ the roof _____ first – there were a lot of broken tiles.

JIM   What about the windows?

HARRY   We [4]_____ two of them _____ , but the others were OK, they just needed painting.

JIM   [5]_____ you _____ them _____ ?

HARRY   No, we did the painting ourselves.

JIM   What about inside?

HARRY   That's almost done now. We [6]_____ just _____ the new kitchen _____ .

JIM   Well, good luck. I hope it all goes well.

Modal passives (review) `SB page 107`

6 ★ **Circle the correct option.**

1 Her face *will never be / will never have been* forgotten.

2 This pie *must be / must have been* heated before it is eaten.

3 The building *might be / might have been* demolished because it wasn't safe.

4 A new theatre *may be / may have been* built soon.

5 Don't throw those old clothes away – they *can be / can have been* reused.

6 The child *shouldn't be / shouldn't have been* left alone – the accident *might be / might have been* avoided.

7 The students *must be / must have been* told the rules before the test begins.

8 By the end of this year she *will be / will have been* seen in three new films.

7 ★★ **Finish the sentences by reordering the words in italics.**

0 I dropped my phone in the bath and the shop says *repaired / be / it / can't*

   it can't be repaired

1 The writing on the notice was so bad *have / a child / by / could / it / written / been*

   _____ .

2 This medicine is for adults and *to / children / given / should / be / not*

   _____ .

3 I didn't recognise her in the play, *dyed / hair / have / her / been / must*

   _____ .

4 You've done that wrong! *red / first / should / been / pressed / button / The / have*

   _____ .

5 Why are you taking your tablet with you? *only / can / used / in / with / places / wifi / be / It*

   _____ .

6 Don't phone the bank yet. *be / questions / website / might / on / Your / the / answered*

   _____ .

7 The vegetables smell awful; *they / have / fridge / should / kept / in / the / been*

   _____ .

8 If I'd told my parents the truth / *stopped / have / money / a / would / month / my / for / been / pocket*

   _____ .

8 ★★ **Complete the gaps with a modal passive.**

1 This TV is working, so it _____ away. (must not / throw)

2 These plastic bottles _____ into all sorts of different things. (can / make)

3 Those old-fashioned dresses _____ by a film star in the 1950s. (might / wear)

4 That picture _____ by my grandfather – he was an artist. (could / paint)

5 This film _____ by millions of people over the coming months. (will / see)

6 The biscuits _____ in an air-tight box. (should / store)

7 This purse _____ here by that old lady. She was sitting on this seat. (may / leave)

8 That old doll _____ by many different children over the years. (must / love)

GET IT RIGHT!
Causative *have*

Learners often make mistakes with word order when using causative *have*. Another typical learner error is the failure to use causative *have*, opting for the active form.

✓ I had my hair cut.

✗ I had ~~cut my hair.~~

✗ ~~I cut my hair.~~

Rewrite the sentences correctly.

1 Joe had fixed his bike at the bike shop last week.

   _____

2 My mum has dyed her hair once a month.

   _____

3 George has had stolen his phone at school. He's furious!

   _____

4 Peter is going check his eyes tomorrow at the hospital.

   _____

5 Ben wants to take his computer in to the shop to upgrade it.

   _____

6 We should have had cut down the tree before it blew over in the wind.

   _____

VOCABULARY

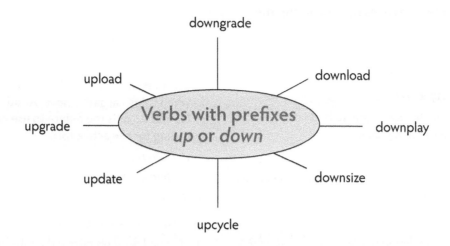

Key words in context

base	Use this cream as the **base** and then put your make-up on top of it.
discarded	There were **discarded** bottles and boxes all over the pavement outside.
hassle	We moved house last week – what a **hassle**! I never want to move again!
heap	There was a **heap** of dirty clothes in the corner of his room.
indicate	The cyclist put out his hand to **indicate** that he was going to turn left.
inferior	If you pay a lower price, you'll always get **inferior** products.
lethal	The chemical factory caught fire and there was **lethal** smoke in the air.
raw material	Did you know that one of the **raw materials** of plastic is oil?
repurpose	The building was a school before, but it has been **repurposed** as flats.
resistant	Farmers use chemicals on plants to make them more **resistant** to diseases.
sack	The potatoes can be bought in **sacks** of 5, 10 or 20 kilos.
scrap	I need to write something down – have you got a **scrap** of paper I can use?
strip	All the information about your credit card is in the black magnetic **strip**.
symptom	People demonstrating in the street is a **symptom** of unease in a society.

(not) getting angry SB page 104

1 ★ **Read the sentences. Did the person get angry or not? Mark the sentences A (angry) or NA (not angry).**

1 I got so worked up that I had to tell her what I thought. ☐

2 I told him what was on my mind – I just had to let off steam. ☐

3 I think I kind of bit his head off yesterday. I hope he's not too upset with me. ☐

4 I'm really proud of the way I kept my cool in that meeting today. ☐

5 I've never seen Jack lose his temper like that before. ☐

6 They just shouted at me for about ten minutes. ☐

7 Fortunately she stayed calm and everything was OK a few minutes later. ☐

8 I didn't like what she was saying at all, but I bit my tongue and left. ☐

9 It wasn't easy to keep the peace between us, but I think I managed to do it. ☐

10 I was late for class again and Mr Bell really had a go at me. ☐

2 ★★ **Complete the sentences with a word from the list.**

shout | cool | go | head | peace | stay
steam | temper | tongue | up

1 Please don't _____ at me like that!

2 I really don't like it when you lose your _____ like that.

3 Just try not to get so worked _____ about unimportant things.

4 The essential thing at times like this is to keep your _____, OK?

5 Sometimes it's helpful to let off _____ .

6 The teacher got really mad and had a _____ at the whole class.

7 Don't say anything! I know it's awful but just bite your _____, OK?

8 Let's do our best to keep the _____ between them.

9 He shouted at her and well, he really bit her _____ off.

10 _____ calm and answer the questions as best you can.

Pronunciation

Intonation: mean what you say
Go to page 121. 🔊

3 ★★★ **Complete the sentences so that they are true for you.**

1 _____ is very good at keeping the peace.

2 _____ shouted at me when I _____ .

3 It's sometimes hard for me to keep my cool when _____ .

4 Once I had a go at someone who _____ .

5 I always have to bite my tongue when _____ .

Verbs with prefixes *up* and *down*
SB page 107

4 ★ **Find eight verbs starting with *up* or *down* in the grid.**

G	E	L	C	Y	C	P	U	D	U
E	O	P	L	A	W	T	D	P	P
D	O	W	N	G	R	A	D	E	D
A	O	C	Y	C	L	A	O	Y	A
R	W	W	I	U	T	Z	W	A	O
G	R	A	N	E	Z	C	N	L	L
P	L	O	P	S	L	E	P	P	N
U	P	G	L	A	I	D	E	N	W
U	P	L	O	A	D	Z	R	W	O
D	R	O	W	L	O	P	E	O	D
U	P	D	O	N	P	L	E	D	A

5 ★★ **Circle the correct options.**

1 My list of contacts is a bit old now – maybe I should *upgrade / update* it.

2 I need better broadband – it's taking forever to *download / downplay* this video.

3 We used the tyres and *updated / upcycled* them to make plant pots.

4 Please use this link to access the documents that we've *uploaded / upcycled* for you to read.

5 It's a very serious situation and we are not going to *downplay / downgrade* it.

6 I decided to *upgrade / upload* the software on my tablet – everything's better now.

7 She was very unhappy when the company *downsized / downgraded* her job, because her pay decreased.

8 Have you heard? They're going to *download / downsize* the staff and we might lose our jobs!

READING

1 REMEMBER AND CHECK **Answer the questions. Then check your answers in the article on page 103 in the Student's Book.**

1 What three things do pedestrians do that annoy Sami Patel when he's walking? _____

2 What two things do pedestrians do that annoy him when he's driving? _____

3 What four things do motorists do that annoy Marina Tomlinson? _____

4 What adjectives do you think she could use to describe motorists? _____

5 What things do cyclists do that annoy Stefan Markowski? _____

6 What adjectives do you think he could use to describe cyclists? _____

2 **This is a blog review of a book called *Too Much Information* by Dave Gorman. Read the text quickly and find:**

1 what other things Dave Gorman has done. _____

2 what the reviewer liked about this book _____

3 what the reviewer's overall opinion of the book is. _____

This week I'm reviewing a book by Dave Gorman.

Like so many other British TV viewers, I've been a long-time, major fan of Dave Gorman's show 'Modern Life is Good-ish', in which he points out some of the absurdities of life in the early twenty-first century. So I was happy to stumble upon his 2014 book *Too much information* (with the subtitle: *Or: Can Everyone Just Shut Up for a Moment, Some of Us Are Trying to Think*). I wasn't aware that he'd written several other books before this one, so my experience of reading him was zero. I approached this one with relish, though, on the basis of the show.

The premise of the book is that in our 'always on' modern society, there is a curse of 'information overload' – we are constantly so beset by bits of so-called information that we end up getting a bit lost. (I say so-called because, as Gorman points out, some of the information is in fact pure nonsense.) Gorman suggests that we need to be cautious and find ways to sift out what's valuable and what isn't.

The book has pluses and minuses. On the minus side, the book uses quite a lot of the same material that I'd already come across in the TV show. I guess I'd been expecting something 100% new and fresh, so somehow I felt a bit misled (not that the title or the blurb really had led me to believe it was all new). The book is nothing more than a collection of pretty short chapters, forty in all, each of which takes some subject that has got under Gorman's skin. Mostly they're funny, and the short chapters mean you can dip in and out at your leisure. But it felt a bit … well, unsatisfying.

On the plus side, however, the book offers some great laughs and, for someone of my generation (born in the mid-60s), a chance to remember how things used to be, for better or for worse. Younger readers might struggle to imagine a world where you couldn't access huge amounts of 'information' just by clicking a button or two and looking at a screen. But Gorman reminds us that it existed, and that in the early days of the Internet, users had to unplug their phone before using the phone line to dial up a connection, meaning you could choose to have access to your landline phone, or to have an internet connection, but you couldn't have both at the same time (and no, you couldn't use your mobile phone instead; they only came later). There's a particularly amusing section where he describes trying to convince his young niece that, once upon a time, TV wasn't in colour, there were only three channels, and the Internet didn't exist – she gasps in stunned disbelief.

His attacks on modern life are not limited to technology, though – he also has a go at 'Greatest Hits' CDs which include songs no one has ever heard of; news stories told in a single sentence; advertising; magazines and … well, you name it really.

So, this was a book I'm glad I bought and that gave me some nice moments on the train home from work. Yet somehow I found it fell short of my expectations. I won't rush out and buy any of Gorman's other books – I suspect they might be very similar to this and to the TV show – but no matter who you are, you'll enjoy at least some things in this one.

---

3 **Read the review again. Mark the sentences T (true) or F (false). Correct the false ones.**

1 *Too much information* is Dave Gorman's second book. ☐

2 Gorman believes that all the information on the Internet is useless. ☐

3 Each chapter of the book deals with something that Gorman dislikes. ☐

4 The reviewer thinks that things were better for his generation. ☐

5 Gorman's niece found it hard to believe what he told her about the past. ☐

6 Gorman attacks two things in modern life other than technology. ☐

4 **Write three questions that you could ask the reviewer about 'how things used to be' for his generation. Then write what you think his answers might be.**

DEVELOPING WRITING

1 **Read Jackie's blog post. Answer the questions.**

1 What three areas did people suggest were better now than in the '80s and '90s?

2 What area of life is more stressful now than in the past?

3 What subject might the writer treat next?

Jackie's blog — just how hard is life these days?

Have you ever wondered what life is like now compared to, say, the 1980s or the 1990s? I went and talked to some people I know who were adults in the '80s and '90s and I asked them – and the answer I got was that overall, life's a lot better now! Which didn't really surprise me, I mean, these days we've got mobile phones and the Internet and so on – but actually, those weren't the things they talked about.

So what did they talk about? For a start, people felt life is better these days because we don't have to work so physically hard since now there are a lot more things like dishwashers to do housework and other boring chores. Then there's the matter of how, these days, it's possible to work at home – and OK, it's mainly computers and stuff that have made this possible, but even so, it means that a lot of people don't have to spend so much of their lives just going to and from work every day.

Not only that, but there's a lot more equality now. The situation isn't perfect, of course, but I think it's easier for all people, whatever their social background, gender, colour and so on, to have equal access to a variety of career opportunities.

That said, it's not all a matter of improvements. Quite a few people told me that they feel more stressed these days because they rely a lot on technology, and they worry about security on the Internet. Plus, we do spend a lot of our time with tablets and smartphones, don't we? One person said: 'Wouldn't it be great to be off the grid for a few days?' Hmm, not so sure about that one! But maybe I'll give it a try – and then write about it on my next blog post!

---

2 **In the blog, find:**

1 an expression Jackie uses to introduce the first thing people talked about. _____

2 three expressions Jackie uses to introduce additional points.

_____

3 an expression Jackie uses to introduce a contrasting point.

_____

3 **In blogs, people often write informally. In Jackie's blog, find and note down at least three more examples of informal language.**

1 the writer uses 'OK'

2 the writer uses 'I mean'

3 the writer uses _____

4 the writer uses _____

5 the writer uses _____

4 **Imagine you are Jackie and you decided to have no Internet connection for five days. What do you think would be the good and the bad points about this? Make notes.**

5 **Write a blog post of about 250–300 words. Start your blog with:**

'OK, I did it! Five days off the grid! Now I'm back and I want to tell you what it was like. ...'

Use some of the language you identified in Exercise 2.
Use some examples of informal language that you found in Exercise 3.

CHECKLIST ✓

LISTENING

1 🔊36 Listen to a radio interview about 'modern teenagers'. Number the things below in the order that the woman mentions them.

2 🔊36 Listen again. Answer the questions.

1 Why is the ability to analyse things increasing amongst teenagers?

_____

2 How has the rate of teenage violence changed over the last decade?

_____

3 How does that rate compare to the rate for older people?

_____

4 Why is an increase in environmental awareness 'to be expected'?

_____

5 What kind of things do teenagers volunteer for?

_____

6 In what way do teenagers now differ from previous generations with regard to their parents?

_____

DIALOGUE

1 Order the dialogues. Then write one word to complete each gap.

Dialogue 1

☐ **MARK** So, don't – just smile and think about something else. Or better, start talking about something else.

☐ **MARK** I get that a lot from my family too. Just don't let it ¹_____ to you.

1 **MARK** What on earth's the matter with you? You look really fed up!

☐ **SONIA** Yes, you're right. But it's not always that easy to smile. I just need to chill ²_____ a bit, I reckon.

☐ **SONIA** I've just been listening to my uncle and aunt going on about how terrible teenagers are these days.

☐ **SONIA** Well I try not to, but sometimes it makes me so mad. And they're nice people – I like them a lot, so I don't want to argue with them.

Dialogue 2

☐ **STEVE** I suppose you're right. After all, there are worse things in life than spam, aren't there?

☐ **STEVE** I suppose not. But sometimes I get so angry that I write back with something rude.

☐ **STEVE** Me too. I hate those emails, trying to sell me something or trying to trick me. It drives me crazy.

☐ **MANDY** I know. But I try not to get angry – there's no point in getting worked ³_____, is there?

1 **MANDY** I seem to be getting more and more spam in my inbox these days.

☐ **MANDY** Oh that's the worst thing you can do! Then they know that your email address really exists. You need to calm ⁴_____ and just hit the delete button.

Dialogue 3

☐ **JASON** Well, that's easier said than done – we're in the same class, so how can I avoid her?

☐ **JASON** It's not what she's done, it's what she's said. Another nasty comment about my sister. She's clearly trying her best to annoy me – and it's working.

1 **JASON** I'm never going to talk to Judy again! I've had enough!

☐ **HARRY** Sit as far away as possible and look in other directions – that's what I'd do, anyway.

☐ **HARRY** Hey, take it ⁵_____, Jason. What's she done?

☐ **HARRY** Look, don't let her get under your ⁶_____, OK?

2 Choose one of the lines below and use it as part of a short dialogue (between 6 and 8 lines).

1 I don't see why you're losing your temper with me!
2 And then she really bit his head off.
3 I tried not to lose my cool, but it didn't work.
4 Don't let them get under your skin, OK?

Reading and Use of English Part 3

For questions 1–8, read the text below. Use the word given in capitals at the end of some of the lines to form a word that fits in the gap in the same line. There is an example at the beginning (0).

Write your answers on the lines below.

Any attempt to compare life in the twenty-first century with that of a hundred years

ago is doomed to (0) _____ . This is principally because, especially in the early part of this   FAIL

century, the rate of (1) _____ change has been so rapid. The things that we use now on   TECHNOLOGY

a daily basis are tools that, for our grandparents, would have been completely (2) _____ .   IMAGINE

Phone technology, in particular, has developed at an (3) _____ rapid rate.   ASTONISH

Almost every day we learn about a new (4) _____ which will offer yet another so-called   INNOVATE

(5) _____ in the way in which we can communicate with each other.   IMPROVE

Yet one might argue that our (6) _____ for such advances, given the levels of poverty   ENTHUSE

and hunger in the world, is (7) _____ . Will we be remembered as the generation whose   JUSTIFY

(8) _____ of technology destroyed our compassion and consideration towards each other?   PURSUE

0 _____*failure*_____	3 _____	6 _____
1 _____	4 _____	7 _____
2 _____	5 _____	8 _____

Exam guide: word formation

In the word formation task you are given a text with eight gaps. At the end of some lines there is a word. You will need to change the part of speech. For example, you may need to change a noun (happiness) into an adjective (happy) or an adverb (happily).

- Occasionally, you will have to produce a negative word from a positive one. For example, you may need to add a prefix to a word (legal) to make it negative (illegal).
- Be careful – sometimes a question will be written in a way where you perhaps will think you need an adjective but in fact you need an adverb. For example, in the question 'It was a … beautiful place' (STUNNING), this would need to be an adverb, 'It was a stunningly beautiful place.'

GRAMMAR

Future perfect; future continuous (review) SB page 112

1 ★★☆ **Write sentences. Use the future perfect or future continuous forms of the verbs.**

This time next year …

1 My brother / still / travel / around / Mexico

_____

2 I / still / study / History / at / university

_____

3 My sister, Helen, / finish / her / degree

_____

4 Helen / still / look / for / a / job

_____

5 My family / move / house

_____

6 We / live / in / our / new / house

_____

2 ★★☆ **Complete the sentences with the future perfect form of the verbs in brackets.**

THE HOLIDAY OF A LIFETIME

By the time you leave Ecuador and the Galapagos Islands …

1 you _____
(hike) up two volcanoes.

2 you _____
(travel) up the Amazon to
remote villages by canoe.

3 you _____ (be)
whale-watching.

4 you _____ (see)
the glacier that covers the
peak of Cotopaxi.

5 you _____
(explore) the famous
indigenous market of Otavalo.

6 you _____
(experience) standing with
your feet in two hemispheres
on the equator line at Mitad
Del Mundo.

7 you _____
(have) the holiday of a
lifetime.

3 ★★☆ **What will you be doing next year? Answer the questions. Write long answers.**

1 A Where will you be living?
   YOU _____

2 A What will you be studying?
   YOU _____

3 A Will you have left school?
   YOU _____

4 A What sports will you be playing?
   YOU _____

5 A Will you have taken any important exams?
   YOU _____

6 A Will you be learning to play any musical
     instruments?
   YOU _____

4 ★★☆ **Use the future perfect or future continuous forms of the verbs below to complete Daniel's six point plan for the future.**

open | think | make | start | complete | queue

I have always loved making cakes. Here is my six
point plan for the future.

0 In five years' time, I _will have opened_ a
   bakery.

1 People _____ up to buy my cakes.

2 I _____ a good profit in the first year.

3 In the second year, I _____ of opening
   a second shop.

4 By the end of the third year, I _____ a
   bread-making course.

5 By the end of the following year, I
   _____ to sell bread as well as cakes.

5 ★★★ **Write a six point plan like Daniel's.**

In ten years' time …

1 _____

2 _____

3 _____

4 _____

5 _____

6 _____

Future in the past SB page 115

6 ★★ Complete the sentences with *was/wasn't/were going to* or *would/wouldn't*.

I had lots of plans for this Saturday. I ¹_____ (play) football in the morning. Then my friends and I ²_____ (have) pizza at a nearby restaurant. Then after lunch, I ³_____ (do) some guitar practice. My friend Tim said he ⁴_____ probably _____ (come) and practise with me. However, I didn't think he ⁵_____ (have) time, as he's got lots of homework to do this weekend. In the evening, I ⁶_____ (see) a film with my sister. My brother ⁷_____ (go) to the cinema too but he ⁸_____ (not see) the same film. He and I ⁹_____ (not want) to see the same film. Then, maybe after the film, we ¹⁰_____ (go and get) something to eat together.

Now here I am in hospital with a broken leg so I won't be doing any of those things!

7 ★★ Rewrite the sentences. Use *was/were going to* or *would*.

0 I wanted to go to the show last night. I couldn't go because it was cancelled.

I was going to go to the show last night but it was cancelled.

1 Martin intended to call you this afternoon but then he forgot.

_____

2 Helena had booked to go on a climbing holiday next week. Now she can't go because she's broken her leg.

_____

3 Dad expected you to be late home but not this late.

Dad thought _____ probably _____.

4 We planned to visit some friends in Spain this summer but then they came to visit us instead.

_____

5 I didn't expect to pass the Physics exam so I was surprised when I did.

I didn't think _____.

6 They hadn't planned to volunteer at the school but now they are glad they did.

_____

7 I didn't expect my little cousin to learn to read so quickly.

I didn't think _____.

8 ★★★ Have you ever made plans and then had to break them? Write some of your plans here. Use *was/were going to*.

I was going to go to university but then I got offered an apprenticeship at an advertising firm. My brother and I were going to have a piano lesson last night but we missed the bus.

1 _____

2 _____

3 _____

4 _____

5 _____

GET IT RIGHT!
Future continuous and future perfect

Learners often use the future simple when the future perfect or future continuous is required.

✓ *This time next year I **will be doing** a degree in English at Cambridge University.*

✗ *This time next year I will do a degree in English at Cambridge University.*

✓ *This time next year I **will have finished** my school exams and be at university.*

✗ *This time next year I will finish my school exams and be at university.*

Rewrite the sentences about the future in a more appropriate form – future continuous or future perfect.

1 I won't be at the lecture tomorrow. Perhaps the day after tomorrow I can borrow your notes on what you will do tomorrow.

_____

2 All of next week we will campaign for the fight against child poverty.

_____

3 By next Saturday the final candidates will be shortlisted.

_____

4 The moment Eve appears on stage tomorrow her lifelong ambition will be fulfilled.

_____

5 Next Tuesday the whole country will vote in the general election.

_____

6 I will lie on the beach and relax this time next month.

_____

VOCABULARY

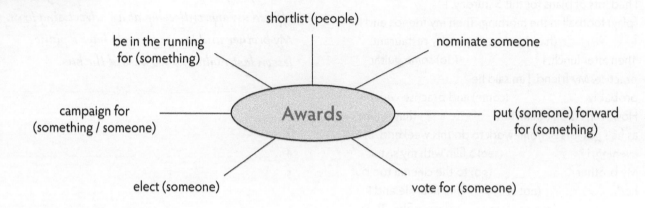

shortlist (people)

be in the running for (something)

nominate someone

campaign for (something / someone)

Awards

put (someone) forward for (something)

elect (someone)

vote for (someone)

Success and failure

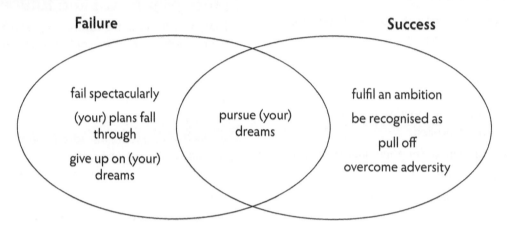

Failure

fail spectacularly

(your) plans fall through

give up on (your) dreams

pursue (your) dreams

Success

fulfil an ambition

be recognised as

pull off

overcome adversity

Expressions with *in*

in the circumstances
in the public eye
in spite of
in no time
in particular
in mind

Key words in context

breathtaking	The view from the top of the mountain was **breathtaking**. It's possibly the best view I've ever seen.
choke	I **choked** on a piece of bread last night. It was awful. It was stuck in my throat and I couldn't breathe.
eternally	I will be **eternally** grateful to my parents for buying me my first violin and encouraging me to pursue a career in music.
grumpy	Jim's in a bad mood again but then he's always a bit **grumpy** when he first gets up.
hysterically	The shock had been too much for Susie and she was crying **hysterically**.
initiative	There is a new council **initiative** to set up a football training centre in every neighbourhood park.
integrate	It is always difficult to **integrate** a new member into the team. We all have to get used to his style of playing.
miracle	It was such a terrible car crash, we thought he was going to die. It really is a **miracle** he survived.
plight	Jamie was in great danger. Luckily he wasn't aware of the **plight** he was in and the rescue helicopter was on its way.
trauma	Gemma is still suffering after the **trauma** of her father's death.

Awards SB page 112

1 ★★ **Complete the dialogues with the correct form of the verbs.**

be in the running for | nominate | campaign for
shortlist | put forward for | vote for | elect

1 A I _____ your name _____ the local environmental hero award.

 B Really? But I don't think I stand a chance. There are so many other candidates.

2 A Leyla _____ the Green party last year.

 B Yes, I heard she delivered leaflets and she knocked on people's doors and talked to them.

3 A Who did you _____ in the election?

 B Tom Jackson but he _____. He didn't win many votes unfortunately.

4 A Did you know Tony Smithson _____ the director's post?

 B Yes, I did. He told me he _____. Apparently they've chosen five candidates to interview out of the 15 applicants.

5 A Who did you _____ for the Henry Moore Sculpture Award?

 B You, actually. I think you've done some great work this term.

Success and failure SB page 113

2 ★★ **Choose the correct phrases.**

1 A Has Alex done that motorcycle stunt yet?

 B No, he hasn't. It's a very difficult stunt to *fulfill his ambition / pull off.*

2 A Did you manage to climb Ben Nevis last weekend?

 B Yes, I *fulfilled my ambition of / was recognised as* climbing the highest mountain in the UK.

3 A Did the stuntman jump over ten buses on his motorcycle?

 B No, he *failed spectacularly / pulled it off* but luckily he wasn't hurt.

4 A Is Mike still going to Mexico this winter?

 B No, *he didn't give up on his dream / his plans fell through.* He couldn't raise enough money for the trip.

5 A Does Debbie still want to swim across the English Channel?

 B Yes, she does. She *has fulfilled her ambition / hasn't given up on her dream* yet.

6 A Antonio has done really well, hasn't he?

 B Yes, he *is recognised as / plans fell through* one of the most talented young divers in the UK.

3 ★★★ **Write a sentence about each of the following.**

1 (an ambition you have fulfilled)

_____

2 (a dream you would like to pursue)

_____

3 (something you have failed spectacularly at)

_____

WordWise

Expressions with *in* SB page 117

4 ★★ **Complete the mini-dialogues with the words in the list.**

circumstances | eye | spite | time
particular | mind

1 A Is it this colour in _____ that you want or shall I show you the shirt in another colour?

 B No, I just want the shirt in this colour.

2 A I've just heard, two of the players, Mike and Jamie can't get here because of the bad weather.

 B Yes, that's right, and the storm's getting worse now. In the _____, I think we should cancel the match.

3 A It must be very difficult to be a famous actor. I'd hate to be in the public _____ all the time.

 B Oh, really? I think I'd quite enjoy it.

4 A Is this the kind of day out you had in _____?

 B Yes, it is. I've loved every minute of it. Thank you so much for organising it.

5 A Did you have a good holiday?

 B Yes, thanks. In _____ of the weather we had a great time.

6 A Do you think you can mend my bike for me? I've got to be home by 5 pm.

 B No worries. We'll have it ready for you in no _____.

Pronunciation

Shifting word stress
Go to page 121.

READING

1 **REMEMBER AND CHECK** Read the online posts on page 111 of the Student's Book again. Then answer the questions.

1 What did Nabeel Yasin hope to achieve by setting up football teams in war-torn Iraq?

_____

2 What values does FC Unity promote?

_____

3 What has Yvonne Bezerra devoted her life to?

_____

4 As well as giving children an education, what else do Yvonne's schools provide for them?

_____

5 What was Saur Marlina Manurung's dream?

_____

6 What can the Orang Rimba do now that they can read and write?

_____

Overcoming adversity

From Pennsylvania farm girl to true heroine of American microbiology, Alice Catherine Evans (1881–1975) made one of the most medically important discoveries of the 20th Century. Unable to afford college, she started her career in 1901 as an elementary school teacher. But when Cornell University offered a free class on nature to rural teachers, Alice jumped at the chance and the course of her life (and history) subsequently changed.

While taking that nature class, Alice also took a basic course in the Agricultural College, which started her interest in bacteriology. She went on to win a scholarship to Cornell, earning her a Bachelor of Science degree in bacteriology in 1909 and then a Master of Science degree in the same field from the University of Wisconsin in 1910. Alice then got a job in the Dairy Division at the U.S. Department of Agriculture Bureau.

Her work at the bureau involved investigating bacteria in milk and cheese. When her appointment was made permanent in 1913, Alice became the first woman scientist to have a permanent appointment in that division of the USDA.

In 1918, through her pioneering research, she was able to show that drinking raw (unpasteurised) milk could transmit the bacterium, Bacillus abortus, which caused brucellosis (known as Malta fever), an infectious disease passed from domestic farm animals to humans. As a result, Alice passionately advocated for the pasteurisation of milk to effectively kill this disease-causing bacterium.

However, her findings and recommendations were not taken seriously by other scientists for two reasons: 1) she was a woman and 2) she didn't have a PhD.

But by the late 1920s, other scientists eventually came to the same conclusion as Alice, and by the 1930s, the government passed laws requiring that milk be pasteurised to prevent the disease. So while it took power in numbers to effect change, it was Alice's discovery that hastened the spread of the pasteurisation movement and, as a result, saved countless people from fever and death.

Ironically and sadly, Alice herself contracted chronic brucellosis in 1922, as a result of her research. She suffered from recurrent bouts for years because the disease never left her system.

After leaving the Department of Agriculture, Alice worked for the U.S. Hygienic Laboratory where she made valuable contributions in the field of infectious illness, including meningitis and throat infections. In 1928, she became the first woman president of the Society of American Bacteriologists (now the American Society for Microbiology). She died in 1975 at the age of 94, and was added to the National Women's Hall of Fame in 1993.

2 **Read the article quickly and find out the significance of these dates.**

1 1909 _____

2 1918 _____

3 1922 _____

4 1928 _____

5 1993 _____

3 **Read the article again. Complete the profile of Alice Catherine Evans. Write a short summary of her career.**

Nationality: [1]_____

Profession in early life: [2]_____

Profession in later life: [3]_____

University qualifications: [4]_____

Major discovery: [5]_____

Valuable contributions: [6]_____

Summary (maximum of 75 words):

_____

_____

_____

4 **Can you find another scientist who was not acknowledged at the time of their scientific research? Do some research. Write a profile for them.**

DEVELOPING WRITING

A blog post

1 **Read Jamie's blog about an invention he admires. Then answer the questions.**

1 What did Martin Cooper invent?

2 Is his invention cheaper today or more expensive?

2 **Read and complete the sentences about Martin Cooper and his invention.**

1 He didn't know half the people in the world _____.

2 He didn't know he _____ the world.

3 He had no idea his invention _____.

4 He never imagined the battery _____.

3 **Match the summaries to the paragraphs.**

Paragraph 1
Paragraph 2
Paragraphs 3 & 4
Paragraph 5

a explains things the inventor didn't know would happen.

b tells us what the invention is.

c predicts how the invention will change in the future.

d gives us biographical information about the inventor.

4 **Write a blog of 300–350 words on an invention you admire.**

- What is the invention? e.g. the Internet, robots, planes.

- Who played their part in inventing it? Choose one person. Are they an unsung hero or are they well-known?

- Give a short biography of the inventor.

- What did they <u>not</u> know would happen to their invention?

- Use your imagination. How will the invention change in the future? What do you think?

Martin Cooper – who's he?

You've probably never heard of Martin Cooper, but he's invented something that half the people on the planet carry around with them every day. It sits on tables in restaurants. It rings unexpectedly in cinemas and theatres. It keeps you in touch with family, friends and the whole wide world 24 hours a day. I'm sure you've guessed now what it is – a mobile phone.

Martin Cooper was born on 26th December, 1928, in Chicago in the USA. As a child he took things apart and invented things. He always wanted to know how things worked. In 1950, he graduated from the Illinois Institute of Technology, and then he joined the U.S. Naval Reserves, where he served on a submarine.

In 1973, Martin Cooper didn't know that he was going to change the world. But then he and his team at Motorola created the mobile phone. That first phone cost Motorola $1 million to make. It was the size of a brick and it weighed 2 kg. When Martin Cooper stood on a New York street and made the first phone call, he had no idea it would become so successful.

The mobile phone wasn't sold to the public for another ten years. Then, when it first went on sale, it cost $4,000 to buy, and it was very heavy. In fact, it was the battery that was heavy. The battery weighed four or five times more than the phone and it only lasted twenty minutes. At that time, Cooper never imagined that 35 years later mobile phones would be so cheap. And he never imagined that the battery would last for days.

And what of the future? Martin Cooper doesn't think we'll be carrying a mobile phone in the future. He believes the mobile phone of the future will be placed under our skin behind our ear with a very powerful computer which will be our slave. What do you think?

CHECKLIST ✔

LISTENING

1 🔊39 **Listen to the dialogue and answer the questions.**

1 What is Joe really into?
2 Who is Sam fascinated by?
3 Write the name, Sam or Joe, under the photo that shows where they are going on holiday.

1 _____ 2 _____

2 🔊39 **Listen to the dialogue and write (T) True, (F) False or (DS) Doesn't say.**

By the time they get back from their holidays …

1 Sam will have visited a place of historical interest. ☐
2 Sam will have eaten lots of amazing food. ☐
3 Sam will have climbed the 365 steps to the top of El Castillo. ☐
4 Joe will have climbed an inactive volcano. ☐
5 Joe will have seen wildlife you can't see anywhere else in the world. ☐
6 Joe will have fed the sea lions. ☐
7 Joe will have snorkelled with iguanas. ☐
8 both Sam and Joe will have had fantastic adventures. ☐

DIALOGUE

1 **Complete the dialogues with phrases in the list.**

This time tomorrow, I'll be | It's going to be amazing
I'm so excited about | I'm really looking forward to
He's dying to | it can't happen soon enough

Dialogue 1

SARAH   Mum's booked a trip to Paris for the weekend.

MAX   Oh cool. You've been there before though haven't you?

SARAH   Yeah. It's my little brother, Oscar's birthday.
¹_____ see the Eiffel Tower.

MAX   Right, and what about you?

SARAH   ²_____ going too. I want to go to Montmartre.

Dialogue 2

JULIA   ³_____ in Los Angeles. Can you believe it?

EMMA   You've been talking about it so much. How could I forget?

JULIA   I can't help it. ⁴_____ finally going to Disneyland.

Dialogue 3

MARIO   Are you ready for our expedition tomorrow?

MANUEL   Of course. ⁵_____.

MARIO   I know. I can't wait. Finally we're going to see what's inside those caves.

MANUEL   I know. We've done so much training for it. All I can say is – ⁶_____.

2 **Now write a new dialogue. Talk to a friend about a dream holiday you are going to go on. Use phrases from Exercise 1.**

PHRASES FOR FLUENCY

SB page 117

1 **Complete the phrases with the words in the list.**

fancy | weird | ages | know | like | question

1 What's not to _____ ?
2 What do you _____ doing?
3 I haven't seen you for _____ .
4 How _____ is that?
5 How should I _____ ?
6 The _____ is, …?

2 **Put the dialogue in order.**

☐ CAROL   Of course! The 23rd of April. How weird is that?

[1] CAROL   Hi, Adele. I haven't seen you for ages.

☐ CAROL   Yes, there is. There's a new James Bond film on. Do you like Bond films?

☐ CAROL   I'd like that. What do you fancy doing?

☐ ADELE   We could go to the cinema. The question is, what's on? I don't think there's anything good on this week.

☐ ADELE   I know, it's really strange, isn't it? Listen. We should go out some time.

☐ ADELE   No, we haven't seen each other since Helen's last birthday. And guess what! It's Helen's birthday today.

☐ ADELE   Of course. What's not to like? Lots of action – lots of Daniel Craig!

Reading and Use of English Part 8

You are going to read an article in which five people give their opinions on what it is to be a hero. For statements 1–10, choose from the people A–E. Each person may be chosen more than once.

What is a hero?

We asked you to tell us what you think a real hero is. Here's what you told us.

Person A

What is a hero? I think there are many answers to this question. What I think and you think may be completely different. But for me the defining quality of a hero is strength – not just physical strength but also strength of character. A hero is somebody who saves other people from danger. A hero is somebody very brave who won't think twice about their actions if they see a fellow citizen in distress. Picture somebody running into a burning building to save another person's life – that's a truly heroic act.

Person B

My heroes are all sports people, probably because I'm a keen athlete myself. My hero might be a racing driver, a cyclist or a football player. They must be, however, definitely somebody I can support, somebody whose life I can follow and feel involved with albeit from afar. I can feel happy for them when they succeed and I can feel sorry for them when they fail. I admire them for their sporting achievements. They give me hope that I might one day be as successful as they are. This is what their success says to me – Never give up on your dreams.

Person C

Heroism for me is a quality that you simply can't find in humans. We need to look to fiction to find examples of true heroes. My passion in life are comics and in particular superhero comics. In these comics we find examples of true heroes and the best of the lot is Iron Man. Iron Man used his engineering skills to develop a hi-tech metal suit to help him combat evil. I admire him because he uses his skills to do good. He's a brilliant mechanical engineer and a very good businessman. He's not perfect but he does his best to defeat evil. He wants the world to be a better place. What's not to like about that!

Person D

I think a true hero needs to be creative and through their creativity they have the power to move us with their words or art. Think of those novels that you have read that have taken you to other places, think of those paintings you have seen and that have made you stand back in admiration. The people who create these are heroes. They are driven by an inner force as they try to make sense of our world and pass on their discoveries to the rest of us. They have the power to change our emotions through their art. Can there be anything more heroic than that?

Person E

For me a hero starts out as somebody ordinary. Somebody in fact just like you or me. They are transformed into heroes when their lives are turned upside down by a tragic occurrence and they are forced to call upon inner powers they never knew they had in order to deal with the consequences. They are the survivors of illness or catastrophic natural disasters. They have survived a very difficult situation and shown great courage. But they don't let such events bring them down. They rise above with a fight and determination to carry on. Through adversity they have become stronger.

1 Heroes can potentially be anyone. ☐

2 A hero is shaped by how they react to things out of their control. ☐

3 Not everybody's idea of a hero is the same. ☐

4 A hero is someone you aspire to be. ☐

5 Heroes should challenge our emotional responses. ☐

6 A hero is somebody who is not afraid to face danger in order to help people. ☐

7 Heroes can be flawed. ☐

8 A hero looks to improve the world. ☐

9 Heroes are driven by a questioning of their environment. ☐

10 It's impossible for normal people to be heroes. ☐

CONSOLIDATION

LISTENING

1 🔊40 **Listen to the conversation between Owen and Tina. Who has Owen 'unfriended' on Facebook?**

2 🔊40 **Listen again and choose the correct answers.**

1 What does Tina initially think about the idea of unfriending special friends on Facebook?
   A It's a great idea.
   B It doesn't make any sense.
   C It's a bit of an overreaction.

2 When it comes to communication, what are partners who are also Facebook friends at risk of doing?
   A Talking about their posts too much when they are together.
   B Falling out over things they've posted.
   C Relying too much on Facebook to share their thoughts and experiences.

3 Why might some partners fall out over posting family photos online?
   A Because one of them might think it is invading their or their family's privacy.
   B Because sometimes it feels like they've taken certain photos with Facebook in mind.
   C Because they can't agree which photos to upload.

4 Why might some people not want to know everything about their partner's life?
   A Because they like to keep an element of mystery within their relationship.
   B Because the exact details are a bit boring.
   C Because they haven't got enough time to read it all.

GRAMMAR

3 **Complete the sentences using three to six words including the given word.**

1 Someone broke into our car last night. (GOT)
   Our _____ last night.

2 The workmen are installing a new kitchen for us. (INSTALLED)
   We are _____ .

3 You must report any accidents to the head office. (BE)
   All _____ to the head office.

4 My exams finish on Monday morning. (AFTERNOON)
   By Monday _____ .

5 The film I'm going to starts at 9 pm and lasts two hours. (WATCHING)
   At 9.30 pm, I _____ a film.

6 I intended to phone you but I forgot. (GOING)
   I _____ but I forgot.

VOCABULARY

4 **Choose the correct options.**

1 I really didn't want to *lose / drop* my temper so I just *bit / held* my tongue and said nothing.

2 I'm not going to *vote / nominate* Brian for the position because I'm thinking of putting *me / myself* forward.

3 I'm going to vote *in / for* Ian because he's campaigning *on / for* a shorter school day.

4 Lauren clearly needed to *let / put* off some steam and she ended up having a *go / fight* at me.

5 I didn't manage to pull it *up / off* and *failed / passed* the exam spectacularly.

6 Olivia is in the *chance / running* for the prize and she's on the *small list / shortlist*.

7 Try to stay *peaceful / calm* and not get so worked *out / up*.

8 She never gave *over / up* on her dreams and *fulfilled / completed* her ambition of being an author.

5 **Complete the sentences with missing verbs.**

1 Now their children have left home, they're going to d_____ and move to a smaller house.

2 I only asked you if I could borrow your phone. You don't need to b_____ my head off.

3 Your virus protection isn't very good. You need to u_____ it to a better one if you really want to keep your computer safe.

4 His life wasn't easy and he had to o_____ a lot of adversity to get where he is today.

5 I've just finished u_____ all the holiday photos online if you want to check them out.

6 Their plans to open a vegetarian restaurant have all f_____ through unfortunately.

7 The earthquake was d_____ to a 3.5 on the Richter scale.

8 If she annoys you again, just k_____ your cool and ignore her.

DIALOGUE

6 **Put the dialogue in order.**

1	JANE	Oh no!! My mouse has stopped working.
	JANE	Very funny. Just fix it will you?
	JANE	How should I know when? I just turned the computer on and it was broken.
	JANE	It just won't respond. How weird is that? It's just died on me.
	JANE	What? Can you fix it?
	JANE	OK, but you won't be able to fix it. You're just wasting your time.

	ROB	It isn't actually broken. I know what's happened.
	ROB	I can. The question is – should I?
	ROB	Calm down. What's the problem exactly?
	ROB	Maybe I am but I can try. Now let me see. When did it stop working exactly?
	ROB	OK, this button here on the side is switched off. You just need to switch it to on.
	ROB	Computer mice don't just die. Let me have a look.

AMAZING PEOPLE: Juan Pablo Culasso

Uruguayan Juan Pablo Culasso has never known what it is to see as he was born blind. But not being able to see has not prevented him from becoming one of the top bird watchers in South America. Now, aged 29, he is a leading expert on the birds of South America, having developed an ability to locate and identify each bird by its song.

Juan's interest in nature started at an early age when his father taught him to play bird songs on the piano and took him to the natural history museum where he could handle bird specimens and feel their feathers. At age 12 he began to make recordings of birds and at 16 he was shown how to work a sound recorder and encouraged to go out and make recordings by his teacher Dr Santiago. It was the beginning of a lifelong passion.

Juan spends much of his time walking through the rain forests of eastern South America. He is accompanied by his guide dog Ronja who acts as his eyes and helps him navigate through the dense vegetation. Juan uses his ears to locate the bird then puts on his headphones to help him guide his microphone in the exact direction to get the best recording possible. He has made hundreds of recordings and has released a CD of Brazilian birds called *Welcome to the Atlantic Forest*, which takes the listener through an audio journey of a day in the life of the Brazilian jungle, from before sunrise to after sunset. Juan admits that he did have a problem with colours. He always imagined that the birds with the most beautiful songs were also the ones with the brightest and most beautifully coloured feathers, so he was surprised to hear that in fact the contrary was often the case and that the plainest birds had the most amazing voices.

Juan doesn't think of his blindness as a disability and instead celebrates how this has heightened his other senses. He feels that for sighted people, sound is invisible. He believes that we all have the ability to enjoy it in the way that he does but that that ability is sleeping and we're therefore not tapping into it.

READING

7 **Read the article and answer the questions.**

1 Why are Juan's achievements remarkable?

2 How did Juan get started with his hobby?

3 Who does Juan take to the jungle and why?

4 What is the aim behind his CD?

5 What was Juan's view on the link between a bird's colour and its song? How was it wrong?'

6 Why does Juan think that for sighted people sound is 'invisible'?

WRITING

8 **Which of your senses do you value the most? Write a short text explaining which one and why. Think about the things that you would miss if you lost this sense. Write about 200–220 words.**

PRONUNCIATION

UNIT 1
Intonation: showing emotions

1 Before you listen, read the sentences and predict how the speaker is feeling and the tone he or she might use. Write A (angry), C (cheerful), D (disappointed), E (enthusiastic), P (puzzled) or S (sympathetic) in the boxes.

0 I told you not to tell your brother we were coming here! ☐

1 Why don't we go to London this summer? Let's start making plans now! ☐

2 I'd love to go to the party but I have to look after my little sister. ☐

3 That's funny. I thought I had £20 in my wallet. ☐

4 I'm sorry you're not feeling well. Would you like a cup of tea? ☐

5 It could be worse. At least it's not raining! ☐

2 ◀))05 Listen, check and repeat. Were your predictions correct?

UNIT 2
Different ways of pronouncing c and g

1 Say the words in the list, paying attention to the sounds of the underlined letters. Write the words in the table.

a<u>cc</u>ident | artifi<u>c</u>ial | benefi<u>c</u>ial | bis<u>c</u>uit
<u>c</u>yberspa<u>c</u>e | dangerous | de<u>c</u>ision | disagree
generally | guilty | o<u>cc</u>asionally | regular
suffi<u>c</u>ient | topi<u>c</u> | urgently

/k/ <u>c</u>an	
/s/ <u>c</u>ity	a<u>cc</u>ident
/ʃ/ wi<u>sh</u>	
/g/ <u>g</u>ot	
/dʒ/ <u>j</u>ump	

2 ◀))07 Listen, check and repeat.

Learn the spelling rule:

The letters *i*, *e* or *y* after *c* give the letter a soft /s/ sound. Before *i*, *e* or *y* we keep the hard /k/ sound by using the letter *k* (e.g. *kite*) or *qu* (e.g. *antique*). We can also add *u* after the *c* (e.g. *biscuit*).

This is the same for the letter *g* (e.g. *general*, *giraffe* and *gym* have the soft /dʒ/ sound; although there are exceptions, for example, *get*). We use the letter *u* to keep the hard /g/ sound (e.g. *guilty* and *guitar*).

UNIT 3
Unstressed words in connected speech

1 ◀))09 Listen and read the sentences, putting stress marks above the stressed words in the sentences.

0 If I'd known how to play, I would've joined in.

1 If I had money, I would've gone out for dinner.

2 If she hadn't invited him, they wouldn't have met.

3 If he hadn't missed the train, we'd be having coffee now.

4 A kinder person would've apologised for making us wait so long.

5 We'd still be friends if she hadn't said those things.

2 ◀))09 Listen again and try to say the sentences at the same time as the speaker. You will need to use correct sentence stress to finish at the same time!

UNIT 4
Telling jokes: pacing, pausing and punchlines

1 🔊 13 **Read and listen to two versions of the same joke. In one version, the speaker has not slowed down and paused at all. Which version has been told well, the first or second one?**

A man went to see the doctor and sat down to explain his problem.

'Doctor, doctor! I've got this problem,' he said. 'I keep thinking that I'm a dog. It's crazy. I don't know what to do!'

'Interesting,' said the doctor soothingly. 'Relax, come here and lie down on the sofa.'

'Oh no, Doctor,' the man said nervously, 'I'm not allowed on the furniture.'

2 🔊 13 **Listen again to the version of the joke that has been told well. Write *S* where the speaker slows down and *P* where they pause for effect.**

UNIT 5
Connected speech feature: elision

1 🔊 16 **Listen and read the sentences. Underline the pairs of words where the consonant sound at the end of the first word disappears. There are two in each sentence.**

0 The last person to leave the room must switch off the lights.
1 Millie and Frida came to the house for cake and tea.
2 Julie ran her fastest marathon last year.
3 I lost my ticket and missed the train.
4 She jumped from the building onto the cardboard boxes.
5 He travelled from France to England by boat.

2 🔊 16 **Listen again, check and repeat. Which two consonant sounds disappear at the ends of the words in these sentences?**

UNIT 6
Modal stress and meaning

1 🔊 18 **Read and listen to the sentences, paying attention to the underlined modals and verbs. Circle the one that is stressed.**

0 I (might) come to the football match. Who's playing?
1 Jack might like your help – even though he's very independent.
2 Are you going to Paris too? We could go together.
3 I could tell you the answer, although it wouldn't be fair on the other students.

4 Julie's lost her job; they may have to sell their house.
5 Tom may look young, but he's actually about to retire.
6 It can take two hours to get to that village by train.

2 🔊 18 **Listen again. This time, decide what the speaker is thinking. Tick a) or b), remembering that we stress the modal verb when we are less sure.**

0 I **might** come to the football match. Who's playing?
  a I really want to come to the match. ☐
  b I'll come to the match depending on which teams are playing. ✓
1 Jack might like your help – even though he's very independent.
  a The speaker thinks Jack would like your help. ☐
  b The speaker thinks Jack probably won't want your help. ☐
2 Are you going to Paris too? We could go together.
  a I don't really want to go with you. ☐
  b I want to go to Paris with you. ☐
3 I could tell you the answer, although it wouldn't be fair on the other students.
  a I might tell you the answer even if it's not fair on the others. ☐
  b I don't think I'm going to tell you the answer because it's not fair. ☐
4 Julie's lost her job; they may have to sell their house.
  a It's possible that they'll have to sell the house. ☐
  b The speaker thinks they will probably sell the house. ☐
5 Tom may look young, but he's actually about to retire.
  a Tom looks young but he isn't. ☐
  b Tom looks young to some people but not to everyone. ☐
6 It can take two hours to get to that village by train.
  a It often takes two hours to get to that village by train. ☐
  b If you are unlucky it will take you two hours to get to that village. ☐

UNIT 7
Connected speech feature: assimilation

1 **◀))21 Listen and read, paying attention to the linking sounds. Write the words in the columns.**

~~brown bird~~ | common cold | foreign guest
green pencil | green grass | London Bridge
London cab | thin person

/n/ changes to /m/	/n/ changes to /ŋ/
brow<u>n</u> bird	

2 **◀))22 Listen, check and repeat.**

UNIT 8
Stress in multi-syllable words

1 **Write the words in the correct columns.**

~~anticipated~~ | comfortable | communicative
congratulated | contribution | extremely
fundamental | incomprehensible | materialistic
recognised | undefeated | unrecognisable

Three syllable	Four syllable	Five syllable	Six syllable
		an<u>ti</u>cipated	

2 **◀))25 Listen and check, underlining the stressed syllable in each word.**

3 **◀))25 Listen again, check and repeat.**

UNIT 9
Unstressed syllables and words: the /ɪ/ phoneme

1 **◀))27 Listen to the sentences and put a dot over the short /ɪ/ sound in the underlined words.**

0 The man was released when the police realised it was a case of <u>mistaken</u> identity.

1 They <u>decided</u> they didn't have enough evidence to take the man to court.

2 Mrs Clark suffered a great miscarriage of <u>justice</u> after her children died.

3 The police <u>arrested</u> her for protesting against environmental destruction.

4 I've <u>been</u> worried about him but it turns out there's nothing wrong.

5 The letter in his <u>pocket</u> proved that he had been at the scene of the crime.

6 The police found three <u>bullets</u> at the scene of the crime.

7 They nearly sent her to prison, but <u>subsequent</u> evidence proved her innocence.

8 Many poor people around the world suffer from <u>prejudice</u>.

9 Mrs Clark was <u>convicted</u> of a crime she didn't commit.

2 **◀))27 Listen again, check and repeat.**

UNIT 10
Lexical and non-lexical fillers

1 🔊30 **Listen and write the linking words in the text.**

⁰ *Hmm* . I never even considered going to university. ¹_____, I was always going to go straight out into the world and earn some money. My dad, ²_____ disapproved of my plans. My brothers had both gone to uni and graduated, and I guess it was expected that I'd do the same. To be honest, I was, ³_____, a bit tired of learning. I just wanted to get away from all the rules and regulations and ⁴_____ see what I could do on my own. And ⁵_____ I must confess I wanted to have things like a house and a car. My friends, ⁶_____, accused me of being materialistic. I suppose they were ⁷_____ right, but I don't feel guilty about it. ⁸_____, they've all left university now with massive loans to pay off and ⁹_____ I've got a good job and a fair amount of disposable income. So no, I don't regret not going to university one bit.

2 🔊30 **Listen again and check your answers.**

3 Lexical fillers are real words although they don't have any meaning here except to give the speaker time to think. Non-lexical fillers are words with no meaning. Write the lexical fillers in column 1 and the non-lexical fillers in column 2.

Lexical fillers	*I mean*
Non-lexical fillers	*Er*

UNIT 11
Intonation: mean what you say

1 🔊34 **Read and listen to the same sentence said in two ways. Tick (✓) the sentence where the tone of voice is appropriate and cross (✗) where it is inappropriate.**

0 a I wish you hadn't told her – it was a secret. ✗
   b I wish you hadn't told her – it was a secret. ✓
1 a If you haven't got the time, I'll do it for you. ☐
   b If you haven't got the time, I'll do it for you. ☐
2 a You sound really stressed. Why don't you take it easy? ☐
   b You sound really stressed. Why don't you take it easy? ☐

3 a Don't worry – it's not a problem at all. ☐
   b Don't worry – it's not a problem at all. ☐
4 a Haven't you eaten yet? It's four o'clock! ☐
   b Haven't you eaten yet? It's four o'clock! ☐

2 🔊35 **Listen and repeat the sentences which are said in an appropriate way.**

UNIT 12
Shifting word stress

1 🔊37 **Listen and circle the word you hear.**

	Noun	Verb
0	**con**duct	con**duct** (circled)
1	**con**flict	con**flict**
2	**con**tract	con**tract**
3	**pre**sent	pre**sent**
4	**pro**test	pro**test**
5	**re**cord	re**cord**
6	**sus**pect	sus**pect**

2 Write the word you circled to complete the sentences. Write N for noun or V for verb.

0 Let's all put money in and get Jake a *present* for his birthday. N
1 She was only eighteen when they asked her to _____ the orchestra. ☐
2 They have no proof, but they _____ that he stole the money. ☐
3 He broke the world _____ for the longest solar powered flight. ☐
4 The world is full of _____ ; we hope there will be more peace in the future. ☐
5 When you accept a job, you often need to sign a _____ . ☐
6 They decided to _____ against the trees being cut down in the park. ☐

3 🔊38 **Listen, check and repeat.**

GRAMMAR REFERENCE

UNIT 1
Talking about habits

1 To talk about things that are generally (but not always) true, we can use the verb *tend to* + verb.

*My friends and I **tend to stay** home on cold evenings.*
*It **tends to rain** here in spring.*

2 We can also use the modal verb *will/won't* + infinitive. In this use, *will* does not have a future reference. This use often refers to how we expect people to behave.

*When my sister has a problem, she **will** only **tell** me about it, no one else.*
*Dad **won't let** us leave the dinner table until everyone's finished their food.*

3 When someone has a habit or does something repeatedly, and it annoys us, we can use the present continuous + *always*.

*He's **always phoning** me to ask me out, even though I've hinted that I'm not interested.*
*Our neighbours **are always making** lots of noise. They seem to have a party every weekend.*

4 We often talk about past habits using *used to* + infinitive or *would* + infinitive.

*When we lived in Japan, we **used to eat** more seafood.*
*When she was a child, she **would sit** in her room all day.*

Adverbs to express attitude

We use words like *unfortunately, admittedly, hopefully, understandably, surely, honestly* and *obviously* to show how we feel about the situation or action we're describing. They usually come at the start of the sentence.

***Unfortunately** I can't go to their party tonight.*
***Hopefully** they'll have another party, and I'll be able to go.*

UNIT 2
Past tenses with hypothetical meaning

1 With some expressions, for example, *it's time, I'd rather, I'd prefer (it if), I wish, If only* we use a past tense to talk about how we would like situations to be different.

2 We use *It's time* + past tense to say that something needs to happen soon.

*It's really late. **It's time** we went home.*

3 We use *I'd rather* + subject + past tense, or *I'd prefer it if* + past tense, to talk about how we'd prefer things to be.

***I'd rather** he **didn't** make that noise when he's eating.*
***I'd prefer it if** we **watched** a film rather than the football.*

4 With *It's time* and *I'd prefer* we use the infinitive when the subject of the second verb is the same as the subject of *It's time / I'd prefer*. If the subject is different, we use the past tense structure.

It's time to go. (= I/we have to go now.)
It's time you went. (= I think you have to go now.)
I'd prefer to eat curry. (= I want to eat curry.)
I'd prefer it if you cooked dinner tonight. (= I want you to cook dinner tonight; I don't want to cook.)

5 We use *I wish / If only* + past tense to talk about how we would like a present situation to be different.

***I wish** I **was** at home. (= I'm not at home.)*
***If only** I **didn't** have to go to school tomorrow.*
(= I have to go to school tomorrow.)

6 We use *I wish / If only* + past perfect tense to talk about how we regret a past situation or action.

***I wish** you **hadn't told** me that. (= You told me something I didn't want to hear/know.)*
***If only** I **had listened** to his advice. (= I didn't listen to his advice, but I now think I should have.)*

Adverbs for modifying comparatives

1 To make a contrast stronger, we can use *much* or *a lot/lots*. We can also use adverbs such as *considerably, far, significantly, notably, way* and *drastically.*

*Food is now **significantly** more expensive than last year.*
*Their new album is **way / far** better than the last one.*
*Her health has got **drastically** worse, I'm afraid.*

2 There are differences in register amongst these words. *Notably* and *Significantly* are used in more formal spoken contexts and in writing.

3 To make a *not as … as* construction stronger, we can use *not nearly, nothing like* and *nowhere near.*

*Your bike is **nowhere near** as good as mine.*

UNIT 3
Mixed conditionals

1 If we want to connect a hypothetical (imaginary) past with a present action or situation, then the *if* clause follows the pattern of a third conditional and the consequence clause follows the pattern of a second conditional.

*If I **had caught** the bus, I **would be** at school now.*
(= I didn't catch the bus and I'm not at school yet.)

2 If we want to connect a hypothetical (imaginary) present with a past action or situation, the *if* clause follows the pattern of a second conditional and the consequence clause follows the pattern of a third conditional.

*If his parents **earned** more money, they**'d have paid** for him to go on the school trip. (= They don't earn more money so they didn't pay for the school trip.)*

Alternatives to *if*

1 We can use other words apart from *if* when we want to talk about (real or imaginary) actions and their consequences. Some common ones are: *as long as, otherwise, provided that, suppose, imagine* and *unless*.

2 We use *as long as* and *provided (that)* to mean 'on the condition that'. We use these mainly in first conditional sentences, and usually (though not exclusively) when we are negotiating something with someone.

*You can go to the match **as long as** you tidy your room.*
*I'll tell you a secret, **provided (that)** you don't tell anyone.*

3 We use *imagine* and *suppose* in second and third conditional sentences when we are hypothesising about imaginary (present or past) situations. They are used at the beginning of sentences and are often used to introduce questions.

Imagine you could visit any country in the world, where would you go?
Suppose you knew that one of your friends had stolen something, what would you do?

4 *Unless* has the meaning of *if not*. It can be used in all conditional structures.

*I won't go to the dentist **unless** the pain gets worse. (= If the pain doesn't get worse, I won't go to the dentist.)*

5 We often use *otherwise* when we want to warn someone about what will happen if a condition is not met. We typically use this in first conditional sentences but we can use it in other conditionals too.

*I need to spend less money. **Otherwise** I'll have nothing left by the weekend.*

UNIT 4
Emphatic structures

1 When we want to write or say something with emphasis, we can use a cleft sentence, using *what, it* or *all*.

It's his facial expressions that make me laugh.
What makes me laugh is his facial expressions.
All I know is that he has great facial expressions.

2 We use the word *it* when we want to focus attention on the information at the beginning of the sentence, often to correct what someone else has said or to offer an alternative opinion or idea.

It was Santos Dumont who made the first ever flight, not the Wright brothers.

3 The word *what* is used in this way to mean 'the thing that'. We use *what* in this way when we want to emphasise what comes at the end of the sentence.

What matters to a lot of people is how the government spends public money.

4 If we want to focus on one particular thing, we can use the word *all* to mean 'the only thing that'.

All I want to do is go to bed.

5 The form of these structures is as follows:

What / All + clause + *be* + clause
It + *be* + noun phrase + relative clause

Boosting

1 We use adverbs such as *certainly, undoubtedly, unquestionably* and *definitely* to make what we say sound more certain and forceful. This is known as boosting. Other common adverbs include *undeniably, clearly, absolutely, utterly, entirely, essentially, literally* and *totally*.

*She **definitely** doesn't like me.*
*That was a **totally** amazing concert.*
*Germany were **undeniably** the better team on the day.*

2 Remember the usual positioning of adverbs:

After the verb *to be*:
*It **was unquestionably** the most difficult test we'd ever done.*
Before the main verb:
*They **undoubtedly expected** to win the match.*
After auxiliaries:
*They **have clearly** not understood the instructions.*

UNIT 5
Participle clauses

In participle clauses, we use the present or past participle form of the verb, or the perfect participle, to combine two clauses that share the same subject.

1   We use them to talk about two events that happen(ed) at the same time.
    Taking a deep breath, he jumped into the freezing water. (= At the same time as he took a deep breath, he jumped into the water.)

2   We use them to talk about an action that happened before the other action in the sentence.
    Having arrived at the station, we bought our tickets. (= We arrived at the station and then bought tickets.) NB in this case we use *having* followed by the past participle.

3   Remember, the subject of both clauses must be the same.
    ~~*Walking down the street, a really heavy rainstorm soaked me.*~~ (This suggests the rainstorm was walking down the street.)
    Walking down the street, I got soaked by a really heavy rainstorm. (This sentence is acceptable as the subject (*I*) is the same in both clauses.)

4   With passive structures, we use the past participle.
    Equipped with a parachute, he jumped out of the plane.

5   We can also use participle clauses to give reasons for something.
    Having heard about the new museum, she decided to visit it. (= Because she heard about the new museum, she decided to visit it.)

6   Note that participle clauses are more common in writing than in spoken language.

Verbs of perception with infinitive or gerund

1   Verbs of perception (e.g. *see*, *feel*, *hear*) can be followed by another verb either in the gerund or in the infinitive.

2   If we follow with a gerund, it suggests that we saw (or felt or heard) part of an ongoing action.
    We *heard* a man *shouting* downstairs. (= A man shouted many times and we heard some of it.)

3   If we follow with an infinitive, it suggests that we saw (or felt or heard) a complete action from beginning to end.
    We *heard* a man *shout* downstairs. (= A man shouted and we heard this in its entirety.)

UNIT 6
Modal verbs

Modal verbs each have more than one use / meaning.

1   *Will* and *won't* can be used to state a belief about the future.
    I think we *will / won't* discover life on other planets.
    will can also be used to talk about habitual behaviour in the present.
    He *will leave* his dirty cups without washing them.
    won't can be used to express refusal.
    Their children *won't eat* vegetables, only potatoes.

2   To hypothesise or to talk about present and future possibilities, we can use *may / might / could*.
    Don't touch that – it *could be* dangerous.
    We *may be* home late tonight.

3   *Can* and *may* can also be used to ask for or give permission. Here, *may* is more formal than *can* and so it is less frequent.
    Can / May we *change* the channel on the TV, please?

4   *Can* is also used to talk about general ability, and about tendencies or theoretical possibility.
    They *can be* very rude sometimes. (tendency)
    Temperatures *can reach* up to 40 degrees in Madrid in the summer. (theoretical possibility)
    He *can lift* 100 kg above his head. (ability)

5   As well as talking about present or future possibilities, *could* describes general past ability.
    My grandmother *could speak* six languages.

6   *Should* is used either to give advice, to make recommendations, or to talk about expectations.
    I think you *should go* and lie down. (advice)
    You *should see* that film. It's great. (recommendation)
    You *should ask* before taking something. (expectation)

7   *Must* is used to make a deduction, for strong advice, or for strong obligation.
    You've worked hard – you *must be* tired. (deduction)
    If you go to London, you *must go* on the London Eye. (advice)
    You *must give* it back to me tomorrow. (obligation)

8   *Mustn't* is used for prohibition.
    We *mustn't make* a noise in here.

9   *Can't* is used for lack of ability, or to say that something is impossible, based on deduction.
    I *can't answer* this question. (lack of ability)
    Ninety percent of people pass that test, so it *can't be* very difficult. (deduction)

10 We can also use *might / may* to express concession.
    He *might be* rich, but I don't think he's very happy.

UNIT 7
Substitution

1 In formal situations and sometimes in written English, we can avoid repetition of nouns by using *that (of) / those (of)*. When we are referring to people we must use *those*.

*An important **question** is **that of** the country's economy.*
*Many **people** like fast food, but there are **those** who hate it.*

2 We can avoid repeating verb phrases by using *do / did / think / hope + so*.

*He says they're a great band, but I really **don't think so**.*
A: *Please take these bags to my room.*
B: *I will **do so** immediately, Sir.*

3 To avoid repeating ideas, we can use *so / neither, nor*. The phrases take on the meaning of 'also'. The subject and object are inverted.

*I didn't want to go and **neither did she**.*
A: *I'm looking forward to our holiday.*
B: *So am I!*

Ellipsis

We often leave words out in English. This is known as 'ellipsis' and is especially true of informal spoken language. The words that are most frequently omitted are subject pronouns (*I / you*) and auxiliary verbs (e.g. *do / did / are / is* etc.). When the context is very clear, we often leave out verbs as well.

A *Did you have a good weekend? = Good weekend?*
B *Yes, I had a good weekend. = Yes, I did.*
A *Are you looking for someone? = Looking for someone?*
B *No, I'm not looking for anyone. = No, I'm not.*

UNIT 8
Relative clauses with determiners and prepositions

1 In relative clauses, if there is a preposition, it usually appears at the end of the clause.

*He isn't someone **that** I really want to talk **to**.*
*There's a bridge **that** you have to walk **over**.*

2 However, in formal written or spoken language, we can put the preposition before the relative pronoun. In this case the only two possible relative pronouns are *whom* (for people) and *which* (for things). In normal spoken language, we tend not to use the relative pronoun *whom* as it can sound overly formal.

*There is not a single person here **to whom** I wish to talk.*
*It's a language **with which** he had little familiarity.*

3 Sometimes the relative clause begins with a determiner e.g. *all of whom / some of which / none of whom / in which case*.

*We invited 100 guests to the wedding, **all of whom** came.*
*One of the dishes was a very hot curry, **most of which** was left uneaten.*
*It's possible that over a hundred people will come, **in which case** we will need more chairs.*

however / wherever / whatever etc.

1 We can add *-ever* to *wh-* words to form the words *whatever, whoever, wherever, whenever, whichever* and *however*.

2 When we do this, the result is to create words which mean 'no matter what' (*whatever*) or 'no matter who' (*whoever*) and so on.

***Whatever** happens, don't panic!* (= No matter what happens, don't panic.)
***However** hard I work, I never seem to please the boss.* (= It doesn't matter how hard I work …)

3 *Whatever, wherever, whoever* and *whenever* are normally followed by a verb phrase.

*Whatever **you do**, I'll be happy.*
*Wherever **he goes**, he makes new friends.*
*Whoever **is chosen** for the job will have a great career ahead of them.*
*Whenever **we have** a party, the neighbours complain about the noise.*

4 *Whichever* is usually followed by a noun phrase. *Whatever* can also be followed by a noun phrase.

*Whichever **laptop** I buy, it has to have voice recognition.*
*Whatever **day** you want to have the party, we can arrange it.*

5 *However* is followed by an adjective or adverb.

*However **cold** the water is, we always go swimming.*
*However **carefully** he checked the numbers, he always got a different answer.*

UNIT 9
Negative inversion

1 Sometimes we bring negative or limiting adverbs and adverbial phrases to the beginning of a sentence in order to emphasise something. This is much more common in written than in spoken language but can be used in both for dramatic effect.

2 The word order of the sentence is inverted to follow the pattern of a question. When this inversion happens, we insert the auxiliary *do*, *does* or *did*, and we invert the auxiliary and the subject. With *be* and modal verbs, we use the auxiliary that's already there (e.g. *is / are / can / will* etc.) in the appropriate tense.

He rarely wins a match. → ***Rarely does he win** a match.*
We will never go back to that restaurant. → ***Never will we go** back to that restaurant.*

3 Some of the more common negative or limiting adverbial phrases are: *never (before) / rarely / not only … but also / under no circumstances / on no account / no sooner … than.*

***Never before have I eaten** such wonderful food.*
***Rarely is** a car like that seen on our streets.*
***Not only did you shout** at her, you also made her cry.*
***Under no circumstances are pets allowed** in here.*
***On no account can you** do that.*
***No sooner had we arrived than** he got up to leave.*

Spoken discourse markers

1 We use a lot of discourse markers in spoken language for a number of different purposes.

2 If we want to make it clear that we are talking about a result or outcome, we can use phrases like *as a result*.

*Her arguments were very convincing and **as a result** I changed my opinion.*

3 To show we are giving an opinion we can use a phrase like *as far as I'm concerned, to be honest, to tell you the truth* or *if you ask me*.

***If you ask me**, this government is doing everything wrong.*

4 To show that we're changing the topic of a conversation, we can use a phrase like *by the way*.

*Yes, the concert was great. **By the way**, have you heard the latest CD they've released?*

5 We can show a contrast using a phrase such as *on the other hand, nevertheless* or *that said*.

*She's a great singer. **That said**, her choice of songs isn't great.*

UNIT 10
Reported verb patterns

1 There are many verbs which can be used to report what someone said – for example, *say, tell, promise, suggest, persuade, admit, recommend, apologise*. However, the patterns that follow these verbs vary.

2 Some reporting verbs are followed by (person) + preposition + gerund – for example, *accuse / blame / apologise*.

*They **apologised for** being late.*
*He **accused me of lying** about the missing money.*

3 One very common pattern is *that* + clause – this happens with verbs like *say, claim, tell, argue, emphasise*, etc.

*He **emphasised that** it was very important to read the instructions.*
*She **argued that** I did not have the right to tell her what to do.*

4 Some verbs (for example, *promise, refuse, decide*) are followed by an infinitive + *to*.

*The government **refused to reconsider** its position on the matter.*
*We **decided to take** a ten-minute break.*
*You **promised to tell** me as soon as you heard.*

However, *promise* and *decide* can also be followed by *that* + clause.

*The director **promised [us] that we would** better off under her new plan.*
*They **decided that their dog** should be left outside.*

5 Some verbs (for example, *suggest, deny, regret*) are normally followed by a gerund.

*The fire officer **suggested installing** fire alarms.*
*She **regretted taking** part in the demonstration.*

6 Some verbs (for example, *invite, encourage, advise, warn*) are followed by object pronoun + (*not*) *to* + infinitive.

*They **invited us to join** them on their holiday.*
*I **warned him not to take** my things without asking.*

Passive report structures

1 Passive report structures occur with verbs such as *say, think, believe, know, find* and *consider*.

2 We use passive report structures to report information when the agent is unknown, understood or not important.

*Arabic **is said to be** a difficult language to learn.*

3 For reporting information about the present, the structure is subject + *be* + past participle of reporting verb + *to* + infinitive.

*She **is thought to have** a chance of becoming the next president.*

4 For reporting information (in the present) about something that happened in the past, the structure is subject + *be* + past participle of reporting verb + *to have* + past participle.

*They **are believed to have lived** on Earth tens of thousands of years ago.*

Hedging

Hedging is vague or cautious language that we use in order not to sound forceful or overly certain of something. Phrases that are often used in hedging include: *seem, appear, is believed, thought, said to*; modal verbs like *may, might, could*; and adverbs like *probably, possibly, perhaps.*

*This new version of the app **is said to** be far better.*
*The doctor said that a change of diet **might** help me.*
***Perhaps** it wasn't a good idea to do that after all.*

UNIT 11
The passive with *get*

1   We sometimes use the verb *get* instead of *be* in passive constructions, especially in informal speech and writing.

    *I **got** told off by my mum and dad.*

2   We only use *get* in passive constructions with dynamic (action) verbs.

    *His story **got** (was) published in a newspaper, but it wasn't believed by many people.*

3   We usually use the *get* passive when there is a clear good or bad effect.

    *She **got** injured in a car accident.*
    *I **got** offered a new job in the department.*

4   Sometimes *get* is used rather than *be* to distinguish active from stative meaning of a verb and therefore make it clear that an action is involved.

    *The car **was** damaged.* (= state or action)
    *The car **got** damaged.* (= action)

5   *Get* is also used in passive constructions when something happens unexpectedly or accidentally.

    *The bus hit a lorry and a lot of people **got** hurt.*

Causative *have*

1   This structure is formed with the verb *to have* + object + the past participle of the main verb.

2   It is used to make it clear that another person performs an action for us because we asked them to, or paid them to.

    *I **had** my living room **painted**.* (= I paid a painter to paint it)

3   It is also used when a person (often an unknown person) does something unwanted and/or unpleasant to us.

    *The company **had** its computers **hacked**.* (= the company did not want or ask for this to happen)

4   It is also possible, in informal language, to use the verb *get* instead of *have* – the meanings are the same.

    *I **got** my mobile phone **repaired**.*

Modal passives

1   To form a present passive using a modal verb, we use modal verb + *be* + past participle.

    *These animals **can be found** in several countries in Europe.*

2   To form a past passive using a modal verb, we use modal verb + *have been* + past participle.

    *The wall paintings **might have been painted** more than a hundred thousand years ago.*

UNIT 12
Future perfect; future continuous

1   We use the future continuous tense to refer to an action that will be in progress at or around a specific time in the future. It is formed with *will* + *be* + gerund.

    *This time tomorrow we'**ll be flying** to Lisbon.*
    *Don't phone me next Friday morning – I'**ll be taking** an exam.*

2   We use the future perfect tense when we have a certain moment in the future in mind as we describe / reference an action that happened before that moment. It is formed with *will* + *have* + past participle.

    *At 8 o'clock tomorrow night, our plane **will have arrived** in Lisbon.*
    *By midday next Friday, my exam **will have finished**.*

Future in the past

1   When we want to talk about the future as seen from the past, we can use *was/were going to* or *would*.

    *Last year, I **was going to have** a party for my birthday but in the end, I didn't.*
    *I decided not to have a party because I wasn't sure that people **would come**.*

2   We tend to use *would* or *wouldn't* when we are referring to a future possibility or an idea.

    *I decided not to take the driving test because I thought I **would fail**.*

3   We tend to use *was/were going to* when we are referring to a definite plan for the future.

    *The government **was going to increase** the tax, but people complained too much.*

4   There is more certainty that the future plan or event will take place with *was/were going to* than with *would*.

IRREGULAR VERBS

Base form	Past simple	Past participle
be	was / were	been
bear	bore	borne
beat	beat	beaten
become	became	become
begin	began	begun
bend	bent	bent
bet	bet	bet
bite	bit	bitten
blow	blew	blown
break	broke	broken
breed	bred	bred
bring	brought	brought
broadcast	broadcast	broadcast
build	built	built
burn	burned / burnt	burned / burnt
buy	bought	bought
can	could	–
catch	caught	caught
choose	chose	chosen
come	came	come
cost	cost	cost
cut	cut	cut
deal	dealt	dealt
dive	dived / dove	dived
do	did	done
draw	drew	drawn
dream	dreamed / dreamt	dreamed / dreamt
drink	drank	drunk
drive	drove	driven
eat	ate	eaten
fall	fell	fallen
feed	fed	fed
feel	felt	felt
fight	fought	fought
find	found	found
flee	fled	fled
fly	flew	flown
forbid	forbade	forbidden
forget	forgot	forgotten
forgive	forgave	forgiven
freeze	froze	frozen
get	got	got
give	gave	given
go	went	gone
grow	grew	grown
hang	hung	hung
have	had	had
hear	heard	heard
hide	hid	hidden
hit	hit	hit
hold	held	held
hurt	hurt	hurt
keep	kept	kept
know	knew	known
lay	laid	laid
lead	led	led
leap	leaped / leapt	leaped / leapt
learn	learned / learnt	learned / learnt

Base form	Past simple	Past participle
leave	left	left
lend	lent	lent
let	let	let
lie	lay / laid	lain
light	lit	lit
lose	lost	lost
make	made	made
mean	meant	meant
meet	met	met
overcome	overcame	overcome
pay	paid	paid
put	put	put
quit	quit	quit
read /riːd/	read /red/	read /red/
ride	rode	ridden
ring	rang	rung
rise	rose	risen
run	ran	run
say	said	said
see	saw	seen
seek	sought	sought
sell	sold	sold
send	sent	sent
set	set	set
shake	shook	shaken
shine	shone	shone
shoot	shot	shot
show	showed	shown
shut	shut	shut
sing	sang	sung
sink	sank	sunk
sit	sat	sat
sleep	slept	slept
speak	spoke	spoken
speed	sped	sped
spend	spent	spent
spill	spilled / spilt	spilled / spilt
split	split	split
spread	spread	spread
stand	stood	stood
steal	stole	stolen
stick	stuck	stuck
strike	struck	struck
swear	swore	sworn
sweep	swept	swept
swim	swam	swum
swing	swung	swung
take	took	taken
teach	taught	taught
tear	tore	torn
tell	told	told
think	thought	thought
throw	threw	thrown
understand	understood	understood
wake	woke	woken
wear	wore	worn
win	won	won
write	wrote	written